Tipb
Drums

This publication is not authorised for sale in the United States of America and/or Canada.

Exclusive Distributor for the UK:

Music Sales Limited, Distribution Centre, Newmarket Road,
Bury St Edmunds, Suffolk IP33 3YB, UK.

Typeset in Glasgow and Minion.

Printed in The Netherlands.

No part of this book may be reproduced in any form without prior written permission from the publisher except for the quotation of brief passages in reviews.

The publisher and author have done their best to ensure the accuracy and currency of all the information in the Tipbook, however, they can accept no responsibility for any loss, injury or inconvenience sustained as a result of information or advice contained in the guide. Trademarks, user names, and certain illustrations have been used in this book solely to identify the products or instruments discussed. Such use does not identify endorsement by or affiliation with the trademark owner(s).

© 2007 THE TIPBOOK COMPANY BV, The Netherlands

ISBN 978-1-84772-071-9

Order No. AM990462

www.musicsales.com

Hugo Pinksterboer

Tipbook
Drums

**Handy, clearly written, and up-to-date.
The reference manual for both beginning and
advanced drummers, including Tipcodes and a
glossary.**

Wise Publications
part of The Music Sales Group

London • New York • Paris • Sydney • Copenhagen • Berlin • Madrid • Tokyo

Thanks

For their information, their expertise, their time, and their help we'd like to thank the following musicians, teachers, technicians and other experts: Steve Clover, Andy Doerschuk (*Drum!*), Rick van Horn (*Modern Drummer*), Cesat Zuiderwijk, Fred van Vloten, René Creemers, Ifor Baynes, Dennis Boxem and Erk Willemsen (*Slagwerkkrant*, the Dutch drummers' magazine), Pascale Jansen, Gabriel Laurens (EMD, Brussels), Robin Roetering, Gerrie Spaansen, Hans Waterman, Hans in 't Zand, Rob ter Maat, Piet Klaassen, and the people at Drumland.

Additional thanks go to Steve Clover, Andy Doerschuk (*Drum!*), Rick van Horn (*Modern Drummer*), Rob ter Maat, Piet Klaassen Drum Service, and the people at Drumland for their help and assistance.

Anything missing?

Any omissions? Any areas that could be improved? Please go to www.tipbook.com to contact us; thanks!

The makers

Journalist and musician **Hugo Pinksterboer**, author and editor of The Tipbook Series, has published hundreds of interviews, articles, and instrument, video, CD, and book reviews for national and international music magazines.

Illustrator, designer, and musician **Gijs Bierenbroodspot** has worked as an art director for a wide variety of magazines and has developed numerous ad campaigns. While searching in vain for information about saxophone mouthpieces, he got the idea for this series of books on music and musical instruments. He is responsible for the layout and illustrations of all of the Tipbooks.

Acknowledgements

Concept, design, and illustrations: Gijs Bierenbroodspot
Cover photo: René Vervloet
Editor: Robert L. Doerschuk
Proofreaders: Nancy Bishop and René de Graaff

TIPBOOK DRUMS

IN BRIEF

Have you just started to play the drums? Are you thinking about buying a drum set or cymbals? Or do you want to find out more about the instruments you already own? Then this book will tell you all you need to know about the role of a drummer in a band, about taking lessons and practicing, and of course about drums, cymbals, heads, sticks, hardware, tuning, the history of the drum set – and much more.

A good choice
Having read this book, you'll know enough to make a good choice when selecting drums, cymbals, sticks or drum heads, and you'll be able to easily understand anything else you may want to read about these instruments, either in print or on the Internet.

Start at the beginning
If you have just started playing, or haven't yet begun, pay particular attention to the first four chapters. If you've been playing a while, you may prefer to skip ahead to Chapter 5. Please note that all prices mentioned in this book reflect only approximate street prices in US dollars.

Glossary
In the glossary at the end of the book, you'll find short definitions of most of the terms you'll come across as a drummer. To make life even easier, the glossary doubles as an index.

Hugo Pinksterboer

CONTENTS

VIII SEE WHAT YOU READ WITH TIPCODE
www.tipbook.com
The Tipcodes in this book give you access to additional information (short movies, soundtracks, photos, etc.) at www.tipbook.com. Here's how it works.

1 CHAPTER 1. A DRUMMER?
A drummer is the foundation of a band. A good drummer will make a great band sound even better.

3 CHAPTER 2. A QUICK TOUR
A guided tour of the components that make up a drum set.

11 CHAPTER 3. LEARNING TO PLAY
Is learning to play the drums easy or hard? Do you need lessons? The answers are in this chapter, which also deals with practicing (and how to do so quietly) and reading music.

20 CHAPTER 4. BUYING DRUMS
Why one instrument is more expensive than another, what you are paying for, and where and how to get a good buy – new or secondhand.

26 CHAPTER 5. GOOD DRUMS
What makes a good set of drums? What about shell materials, drum sizes, and hoops? What is a bearing edge and what does it do to the sound? Loads of pointers to finding the best set you can buy.

47 CHAPTER 6. HARDWARE
Everything you need to know about pedals, stands, thrones, and racks.

60 CHAPTER 7. HEADS AND STICKS
Choose the right heads and sticks for your sound, style, and technique.

70 CHAPTER 8. CYMBALS
Tips on selecting and combining cymbals.

78 CHAPTER 9. TUNING AND MUFFLING
A basic manual on getting the best sound out of your drums.

93 CHAPTER 10. SETTING UP AND MAINTENANCE
A blueprint for setting up your set and keeping it in good working order. Includes tips on taking your drums on the road.

100 CHAPTER 11. BACK IN TIME
Drums have been around as long as mankind. A lot of history in very few words.

103 CHAPTER 12. THE PERCUSSION FAMILY
The drum set is part of a massive family; meet some of its members.

107 CHAPTER 13. HOW THEY'RE MADE
A quick look into what making drums, cymbals, heads, and sticks is all about.

111 CHAPTER 14. BRANDS
The main drum and cymbal brands in a nutshell.

117 CHAPTER 15. SETUPS
From basic to extended, four classic setups.

120 GLOSSARY AND INDEX
A glossary for drummers, with lots of extra information. Doubles as an index.

127 TIPCODE LIST
All drum Tipcodes listed.

128 WANT TO KNOW MORE?
Still curious? Information about magazines, books, and the Internet, and about the makers of this book.

130 ESSENTIAL DATA
Two pages for essential notes on your equipment.

TIPBOOK DRUMS

SEE WHAT YOU READ WITH TIPCODE

www.tipbook.com

In addition to the many illustrations on the following pages, Tipbooks offer you an additional way to see – and even hear – what you are reading about. The Tipcodes which you will come across throughout this book give you access to extra pictures, short movies, soundtracks, and other additional information at www.tipbook.com.

Here is how it works: on page 79 of this book you can read about taking off a drum head using two drum keys simultaneously. Right above that paragraph it says **Tipcode DRUMS-014**. Type in that code on the Tipcode page at www.tipbook.com and you will see a short movie that shows you this technique.

Enter code, watch movie
You enter the Tipcode beneath the movie window on the Tipcode page. In most cases, you will then see the relevant images within five to ten seconds. Tipcodes activate a short movie, sound, or both, or a series of photos.

Tipcodes listed
You can find all the Tipcodes used in this book in a single list on page 127.

Quick start
The movies, photo series and soundtracks are designed so that they start quickly. If you miss something the first time, you can of course repeat them. And if it all happens too fast, use the pause button beneath the movie window.

TIPCODE

First, make your selection: Tipcode, chords and fingering charts, or the glossary.

The Tipcode window displays movies, photo series, fingering charts, chords, and explanations of the words used in this book.

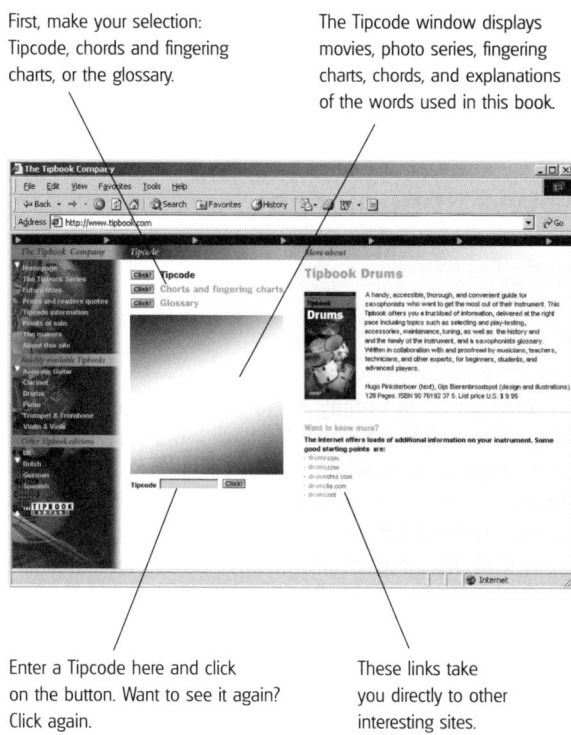

Enter a Tipcode here and click on the button. Want to see it again? Click again.

These links take you directly to other interesting sites.

Plug-ins

If the software you need to view the movies or photos is not yet installed on your computer, you'll automatically be told which software you need, and where you can download it. This kind of software (*plug-ins*) is free.

Still more at www.tipbook.com

You can find even more information at www.tipbook.com. For instance, you can look up words in the glossaries of all the Tipbooks published to date. For clarinetists, saxophonists and flutists there are fingering charts, for drummers there are the rudiments, and for guitarists and pianists there are chord diagrams. Also included are links to some of the websites mentioned in the *Want to Know More?* section of each Tipbook.

1. A DRUMMER?

You hear some pretty wild stories about drummers. They're savages who hit everything in sight. They always play as loud as they can. They can't read (music, that is). And then there's the one about the four-piece band; that's a band made up of three musicians and a drummer...

It's all jealousy, really. Every musician knows that the drummer is the most important member of the band. No band will sound great if there's a lousy drummer up there, and pretty much any band with a great drummer will sound at least acceptable. The drummer is the engine of the band. If your engine's not running okay, you won't get there. It's as simple as that.

Groove
Whether you're into country music, jazz, grunge, soul, funk, R&B or heavy metal, it's always the drummer who gets everyone to start and stop at the same time, who makes sure that nobody speeds up or slows down. Who reminds the singer to come in. Who makes it swing. Who makes it groove. Who makes it feel good.

All musical styles
As a drummer, you can play a wide variety of musical styles. You can play in bands where you need loads of amplification in order to make yourself heard, or in groups where you'll need to play as softly as you can, so the audience can still hear what the unamplified pianist is doing. You can play in big bands or trios, you can play

1

CHAPTER 1

improvised music or music that's written down note for note – and much more.

Easy to learn
One of the great things about drumming is that it's quite easy to learn. You may be able to play a basic rock beat within a couple of weeks, and you'll probably be able to play along to most of the songs in the charts within a couple of months. In the end, however, drums are just as hard to master as any other instrument.

Create your own
Almost every guitar has six strings. Every trumpet has three valves. Every piano looks basically the same. As a drummer, however, you can create your own instrument. You decide how many drums and how many cymbals you use, what your set looks like and how you tune it.

(No) sound
A drum set is about the loudest instrument there is – and yet you can learn how to play the drums without making too much noise. For example, there are special practice sets, you can do all kinds of exercises on pillows, you can play your thighs with your hands, or… More on this is in Chapter 3.

TIPBOOK DRUMS

2. A QUICK TOUR

A drum set is a set of drums, of course, as well as a set of cymbals, and a bunch of stands and pedals, collectively known as the hardware. This chapter introduces you to the main elements of the basic five-piece drum set – which happens to consist of at least ten or more pieces...

Tipcode DRUMS-001

Many drummers use a *five-piece drum set*, 'five' referring to the number of drums in the set. The two main drums are the high-pitched, short and crisp sounding *snare drum* and the low-tuned *bass drum*. The other three are the toms: two on the bass drum, and one on the floor. Sounds familiar? Then just skip this chapter.

Cymbals

Besides those drums, a drum set has various cymbals. The biggest cymbal is the *ride cymbal*, which you use to play the rhythm or the *ride*. Alternatively, you can play the rhythm on the *hi-hat cymbals*, a pair of cymbals, one mounted above the other. You can play the hi-hats either by closing them via a pedal or by playing the top cymbal with your sticks. For accents, you use a smaller, thinner type of cymbal: the *crash cymbal*.

Stands and pedals

Ride and crash cymbals are mounted on cymbal stands, and there is a special type of stand for the snare drum. The two small toms are usually mounted on a tom holder, which in turn is mounted on the bass drum. The bass drum is played with a pedal, as is the hi-hat.

CHAPTER 2

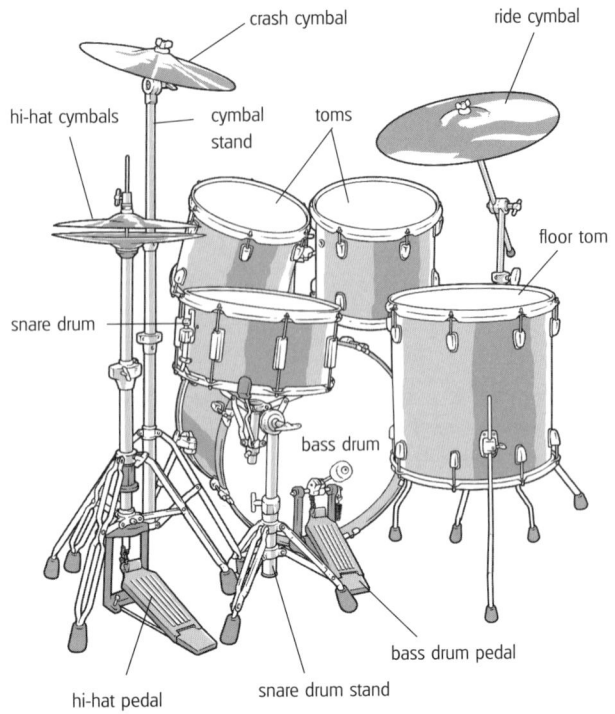

Five-piece set with ride, crash, and hi-hat cymbals.

As big as you like
You can make a drum set as big as you like. Many drummers use one or two extra toms, for instance. Some have two bass drums. And most drummers use additional cymbals: two or three crashes, for instance, one on the left and one on the right, or extra smaller or bigger cymbals. Chapter 15 shows some examples of drum sets, from a four-piece jazz set to a nine-piece rock set.

The shell
The main part of a drum is called the *shell*. This is the sound box of the drum. Snare drums often have metal shells; other drums usually have wooden shells.

The heads
Most drums come with two heads. The *batter head* is the head that you play. Underneath is the *bottom head*, also known as the *resonant head*. If you take it off, you can

clearly hear that the drum sounds less *resonant*; the tone is shorter and not as 'full'.

Rods, lugs, and hoops
You tune a drum head by tightening the *tension rods* in the *lugs*, pulling the *counter hoop* down. This counter hoop, which grips the head by its *flesh hoop*, then pulls the head over the drum.

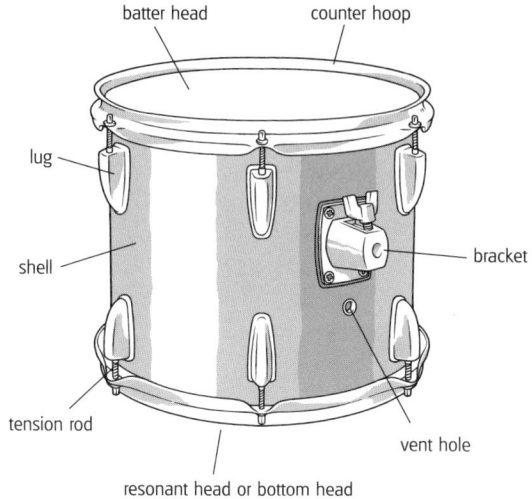

The main parts of a drum.

The main drums
You can play probably ninety percent of all the songs in the charts with just a bass drum, a snare drum, and a pair of hi-hat cymbals. The bass drum and the snare drum provide the heartbeat of the music in many styles, with the bass drum playing every *downbeat* (*one* and *three*), the snare drum every *upbeat* (*two* and *four*): boom, crack, boom, crack... The other drums and cymbals are basically there for embellishment; to play a fill or a break between two parts of a song, to play a solo, or to spice up the basic beat.

The bass drum
Because it is played with a pedal, the bass drum is also known as *kick drum*. It has a low, deep, heavy, and fairly short sound. Most drummers use a 16x22 bass drum; the drum head size is 22", and the shell is 16" deep. *Spurs* on

either side of the bass drum keep it from rolling over or creeping away from you.

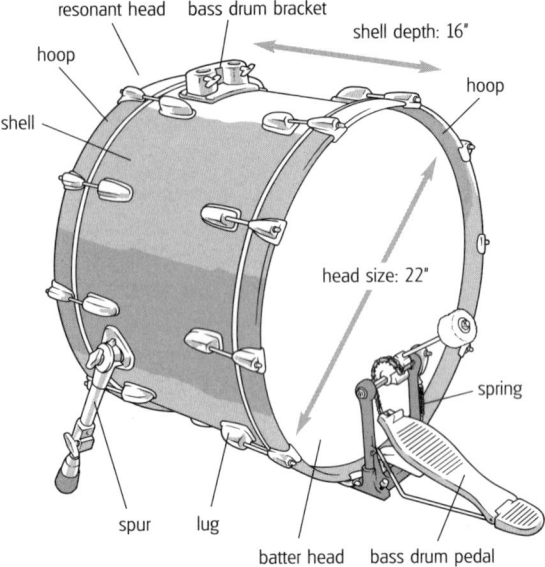

A 16x22 bass drum with bass drum pedal.

The snare drum
Both the sound and the name of the snare drum come from the set of *snares*, consisting of some twenty spiraled metal strands, which is mounted against the bottom head. Every time you hit the drum, the snares bounce off of and immediately snap back to the bottom head, making for a crisp, tight sound. Most snare drums are 14" in diameter, their depth varying from 5" to 6.5". A deeper drum will give a deeper sound.

Snare strainer
A knurled knob on the *snare strainer* allows you to vary the tension on the snares, making the sound a bit tighter or looser. You can use the handle of this mechanism to disengage the snares altogether. Without the snares, the drum sounds more like a high-pitched tom.

Toms
The toms, or tom-toms, are used mainly for rolls, fills, and solos. They come in a wide variety of sizes. The bigger a

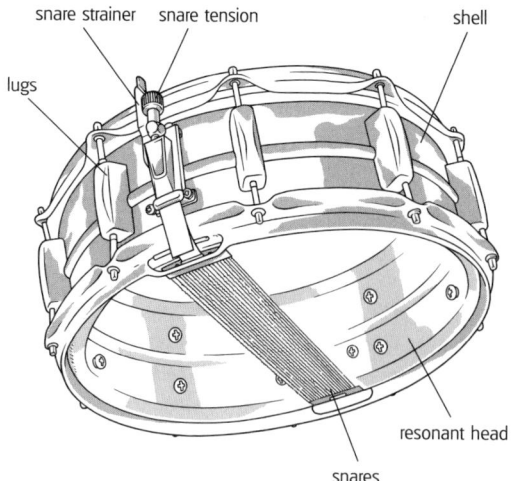

The main parts of a snare drum.

drum is, the lower it can sound. A typical five-piece set has two smaller toms, a 12" and a 13", mounted directly on the bass drum. They're also known as *rack toms*, *mounted toms*, or *hanging toms*. The third tom is the *floor tom*, usually a 16". It stands on its own, next to the snare drum.

Fusion

One of the main variations on this set is known as a *fusion set*, with 10" and 12" toms, a stand-mounted 'hanging' 14" tom, and a 20" or 22" bass drum.

Power toms

Rack toms come in various depths. Traditionally, a 12" tom is 8" deep (8x12). *Power toms* are usually two inches deeper (10x12), and there are also in-between sizes. The deeper a tom is, the deeper its sound will be. Most floor toms have *square sizes*, such as 16x16.

Head first

Drums are usually identified by the head size only: a 12" drum is a drum with a 12" diameter head. If they do specify the depth as well, most American drummers will state the shell depth first. In Europe, they do it the other way around. In other words, an American 10x12 equals a European 12x10. A basic rule avoids confusion: The higher number refers to the head size.

CHAPTER 2

CYMBALS

A basic cymbal set consists of a ride cymbal, a pair of hi-hats and a crash cymbal. The hi-hats are played with your (left) foot, by closing them with the pedal, with sticks or, frequently, a combination of the two.

Keeping time

If you play a basic rock rhythm, you'll play a pattern of beats either on the ride cymbal or on the closed hi-hat cymbals. In other words, you *keep time* on the ride or on the hi-hats. The latter produce a tighter, more defined sound. If you want to hear a more open, sustained type of sound, you may want to use the ride cymbal.

Sizes

Most drummers go for a 20" ride, with the 22" also being quite popular. Other sizes are quite rare. The vast majority of drummers go for 14" hi-hat cymbals, though some prefer a 13" set.

Crashes

Crash cymbals, like toms, are named after the sound they make. And crash cymbals, like toms, are mainly used for adding color to the basic rhythm. They are thinner and smaller than ride cymbals, and respond very quickly, enabling a wide array of accents. If you only have one crash cymbal, it'll usually be a 16" or an 18". If you can afford two, a common choice would be one of each – but there are many other sizes.

Effect cymbals

Besides rides, crashes and hi-hats, there are many other cymbal types, often referred to as *effect cymbals*, from

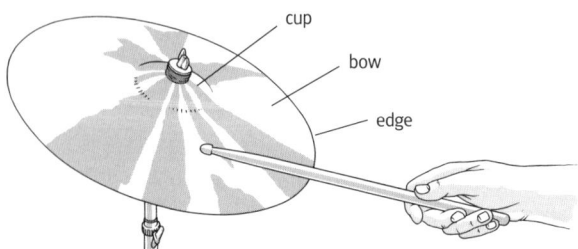

The 'parts' of a cymbal.

paper-thin *splashes* to raw sounding Chinese cymbals. Read more about them in Chapter 8.

Bow, cup and edge
The *bow* of the cymbal is where you hit it when playing a ride. The *cup* or *bell*, in the middle, can be used for tighter-sounding penetrating accents. Crashes are played on the edge, with a glancing motion.

Anything else
Along with all kinds of cymbals, you can add a variety of other instruments to your set, ranging from timbales or the very popular cowbells (see page 104) to tambourines and other small percussion instruments. Chapter 15 shows some examples of drum sets.

STANDS AND PEDALS
The stands and pedals are collectively known as the *hardware*. Most stands come with *double-braced* legs, each leg consisting of two metal strips.

Straight stands and boom stands
Cymbal stands are usually made up of three telescoping tubes. The *tilter*, on top, allows you to angle the cymbal towards you. With the extra arm of a *boom stand* you can position your cymbals anywhere you like. There are also special boom stands for mounting toms.

Snare drum stand
The snare drum is set between the three arms of the so-called *basket* of the snare drum stand. The basket is adjustable to the exact size of the snare drum, and it can be tilted, too.

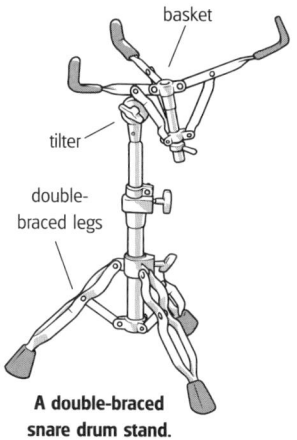

A double-braced snare drum stand.

The pedals
There is a wide variety of bass drum and hi-hat pedals around, some with very basic and others with very sophisticated ways to adjust them to your

CHAPTER 2

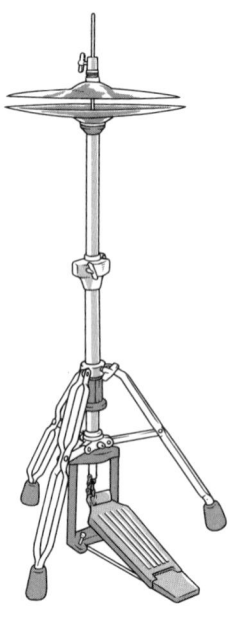

A double-braced hi-hat pedal.

liking. One of the most important pedal adjustments is the *spring tension*, which allows you to make the pedal feel lighter or heavier. The spring of the bass drum pedal is shown in the illustration on page 6. The hi-hat pedal spring is usually hidden inside the lower tube.

Left or right-handed?

If you're right-handed, you will probably arrange your set something like the one illustrated in the beginning of this chapter. Left-handed drummers often set up the other way around, playing the bass drum with their left foot and the hi-hat with their right (see page 96). Setting up this way is not the only option for left-handed drummers; other alternatives are given in Chapter 10, *Setting up and maintenance*.

3. LEARNING TO PLAY

Is it hard to learn to play the drums? Do you have to be able to read music? And what about practicing?

Many drummers are self-taught; they got themselves a drum set, figured out a basic beat and went on from there. Others started out playing just a snare drum for the first year or two, or a practice pad: after all, how can you play five drums if you can't play one? Both ways can be productive.

A teacher
There are many good drummers, and even some great ones, who are completely self-taught. Yet most of the world's top drummers have consulted a teacher at one time or another, rather than trying to work everything out for themselves. Some even still do, occasionally.

What is there to learn?
Good drumming lessons are about more than knocking out beats. They also include subjects like stick technique, posture, rudiments, dynamics, keeping time, reading music, tuning and an introduction to different styles of music. Most important, a good teacher will teach you to play music, instead of 'just' playing the drums.

School or drum corps
Many drummers have their first music lessons at school, and many of them started their drumming careers in a drum corps or a concert band; membership of such a group usually includes lessons.

Locating a teacher

Looking for a private teacher? Larger music stores may have teachers on staff, or they can refer you to one. You can also consult your local Musicians' Union, or the band director at a high school in your vicinity. You may also check the classified ads in newspapers, in music magazines or on supermarket bulletin boards, or consult the *Yellow Pages*. Professional private teachers will usually charge between twenty and fifty dollars per hour. Some make house calls, for which you'll pay extra.

Collectives

You also may want to check whether there are any teachers' collectives or music schools in your vicinity. These collectives may offer extras such as ensemble playing, master classes, and clinics, in a wide variety of styles and at various levels.

First questions

On your first visit to a teacher, don't simply ask how much it costs. Here are a few tips to help you find out whether this is the person you're looking for.

- An **introductory lesson** allows you to see whether it clicks between you and the teacher – or, for that matter, between you and the drums. Asking to sit in on another student's lesson is an alternative.
- Is this teacher still interested in taking you on if you are just playing the drums **for the fun of it**, or are you supposed to practice at least three hours a day?
- Are you expected to make a large investment in teaching books, or are **course materials provided**?
- Can you **record your lessons**, so that you can listen to how you sounded when you get home?
- Is this teacher going to make you **practice rudiments** for two years, or will you be pushed onto a stage to play with a band as soon as possible?

Junior

You can pretty much start learning to play the drums as soon as you can walk, the only problem being that a regular drum set will be too big. There are special affordable junior sets for sale, which can be good enough to start out on. A regular drum set with a smaller (18") bass drum can also be used. Unfortunately, bass drums in this size are not very common in the lower price ranges.

READING MUSIC

Have you ever seen a drummer reading music onstage? Probably not. Yet many of them can read music, and it's not hard to learn. The theory book in this series, *Tipbook Music on Paper – Basic Theory*, teaches you how in a handful of chapters.

Five lines
Tipcode DRUMS-002

Drum music is written in a similar way to music for other instruments, on the same staff. The main difference is that the position of the notes on the staff does not indicate a certain pitch, but a certain part of the drum set: Every part of the set has its own position on or between the five lines. Another difference: The cymbals are indicated by crosses. Here's what it looks like, and with the Tipcode you can hear what it's supposed to sound like.

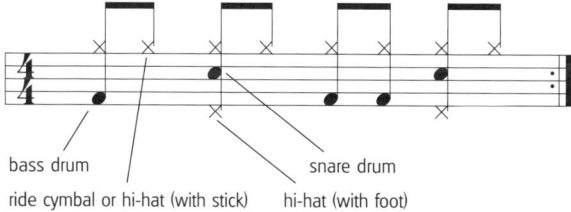

A basic rock rhythm.

Why read?

Why would you learn to read music if you're a drummer?
- If you can read, there are **tons of books** you can benefit from. Books with great ideas for grooves, fills and solos, books with effective exercises, books in which your favorite drummers show you how they did it, and so on.
- If you can read music, **you can also write it**. If you hear or figure out a good beat or a great fill, writing it down is easier and more reliable than remembering it.
- You **won't be lost** if somebody asks you to play sixteenths instead of eighths.
- Reading music makes you **more of a musician**, on top of being a drummer.

- And finally: **Forget all those notes** once you start playing. You'll sound a lot better.

PRACTICING

Drumming makes a lot of noise. What to do about it when you're practicing? And while you're at it, how long should you practice, and what about metronomes and drum computers?

Half an hour

Many top drummers spent up to four or eight hours a day practicing, over several years – or more. If you can't spare that much time, you can make appreciable progress at half an hour per day. The more often you practice, the faster you learn. As with any other instrument, you're better off practicing, say, half an hour a day than a couple of hours once a week.

Less noise

There are four basic solutions to reduce the amount of sound you're bound to produce. Reduce the volume of your instrument, replace your drums with something less noisy, prevent the noise from getting out or, if all else fails, do your practicing someplace else.

Agreed practice times

Lots of musicians keep neighbors and family happy simply by agreeing to fixed practice times.

Muffling your instrument

Stuffing your drums full of rags or cushions will quiet them down, but it takes hours to turn the set into a playable musical instrument again. What's more, even when it's stuffed completely full, the bass drum is still bound to transmit a fair amount of annoyance through floors and walls.

Discs and bands

A much more flexible solution is to use a series of special discs, made of rubbery materials of various hardnesses, that you put on your drums. There are similar designs for bass drums and cymbals as well. A drawback of these discs is that they alter the way your instrument feels; the rebound of your sticks will be strongly reduced. Your cymbals will keep feeling more like cymbals if you muffle them with a wide elastic band. There are commercially available bands made to fit most cymbal sizes.

Gauze heads

You can also replace your regular drumheads with so-called *muffling heads* or *trigger heads*, which feature a very strong type of gauze, instead of the usual plastic film. These noiseless 'gauze heads' or mesh heads, which are also used on some types of electronic drums, offer a rebound that is quite similar to that of a regular head.

Pillows and pads

Unlike other musicians, drummers have a wide choice of alternatives for their 'real' instrument. Playing pillows, for one, has proven to be very effective for many drummers, though there are many teachers who thoroughly dislike the idea. Slightly noisier, but less dusty, is the *practice pad*,

Practice set.

either a single pad or a number of them, set up as a drum set. Practice pads come in two basic varieties: Some have a ply of soft or hard rubber which you play on. Others have a tunable drum head with foam rubber underneath.

Fast rebound
Pretty much all these practice pads produce is the sound of your stick hitting the surface. Most of them have a faster rebound than real drums do – so when you switch back to real drums, they tend to feel slower. Gauze heads feel more like real drum heads.

Electronic drums
Practice pads don't sound like drums. Electronic drums do. Electronic drum sets usually consist of a series of pads or shallow drums with gauze heads which have built-in *triggers*. These triggers convert your playing to electronic signals which are fed to a *sound module* (see page 104), programmed with digital drum sounds. The end result can be very close (or even very, very close) to the real thing. Electronic drums are used a lot in recording studios. Their drawback is that they're still pretty expensive, starting at about a thousand dollars without amps and speakers. Soundproofing a room costs more, though.

Soundproofing
Practicing on a muffled instrument or on pads allows you to work on technique and timing, but it'll hardly help in developing your sound. If you want to practice on the same instrument you play on stage, soundproofing a room is an option. The costs vary greatly, depending on how much you want or need to reduce the sound by, for instance. Making a room really soundproof can easily cost thousands of dollars. Special books on the subject are available. You can also ask other drummers whether they have managed to solve the problem effectively, or find yourself a specialized constructor.

Prefab
As an alternative, you can get yourself a prefab sound-reducing cubicle, available in a variety of makes and sizes. They're easily as expensive as soundproofing a room to the same effect, but you can take them along if you move.

Practicing elsewhere

In most cities there are practice rooms that you can rent for one or more hours – with a band, but also on your own, of course. Many practice rooms come with a drum set, which also may include a set of cymbals, so all you need to bring with you are your sticks. Rental costs are usually quite reasonable. To keep them down even more, you could consider renting a room once a week and using a practice set for the rest of the week.

YOUR OWN EARS

Drumming can be harmful to your ears. Even practicing as little as fifteen minutes a day may cause permanent damage. As hearing loss or damage is usually noticed only when it's too late, prevention is the key.

Cheap or expensive...

The cheapest foam plastic earplugs, available from most music stores and drugstores, will make the band sound as if they're not in the same room with you anymore. The most expensive earplugs, which are custom-made to fit your ears, have adjustable filters, which reduce the volume without affecting the sound.

... and in between

Ear muffs may work well if you don't like to stick things into your ear. Plastic earplugs vary in their sound-reducing effects, as well as in how easy they are to clean. Ask fellow drummers and band members for their experiences, and don't hesitate to try a few until you find the ones that really fit and work for you. A hearing aid will cost more in the long run, and ringing ears (*tinnitus*) never stop ringing.

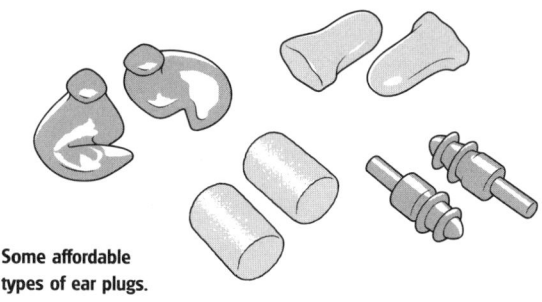

Some affordable types of ear plugs.

CHAPTER 3

DRUM MACHINES, VIDEOS, AND MORE

You can buy all kinds of things to make practicing more efficient, more fun, or even both.

Keeping time

Drummers are supposed to keep time, and to keep the band from speeding up or slowing down. Some drummers have a sense of tempo that makes their time as steady as can be, at every tempo. Most drummers don't. That's where metronomes come in. These small electronic or mechanical devices click or bleep in a steady tempo that you set yourself.

Loud?

A metronome doesn't have to be really loud in order to be heard. As soon as you're a bit off, your hit will not coincide with the metronome's beat; you'll hear the metronome beat, and that'll tell you you're off. Don't go for one that you can hardly hear at all, however. Rather buy one with an adjustable volume level instead. Pretty much every metronome comes with an LED that blinks to indicate the beat, so you have visual control too.

Drum machine

There are also special metronomes for drummers, with a variety of built-in sounds, and even with programming facilities, allowing you to store the tempos of a number of

... a special drummer's
metronome, programmable, with extra power and sounds (Tama).

songs. These metronomes can also play at higher volume levels. As an alternative you can use a *drum machine* or a similar device. They're more expensive of course, but they're more flexible too, they have more sounds (programmable bass patterns, for example), and so they're nicer to work with. Phrase trainers are great practice devices too; they can slow down a musical phrase from CD, for example, enabling you to figure out even the meanest, fastest licks at your own tempo. There is computer software available that does the same thing.

Books, Videos, and CDs
There's a lot you can learn from books, videos, and CDs.
- **Drum books** come in many types and formats, for drummers at every level. Quite a lot of them include tapes or CDs with examples or play-along exercises. Drummers' magazines offer practice material too.
- There are loads of **drum videos**, most of them made by well-known drummers who show you their tricks of the trade. These videos usually last anywhere from thirty to ninety minutes. Booklets with printouts of the recorded rhythms and exercises are not always included.
- **Regular CDs** are great for practicing. Play a CD of your favorite band, put on a pair of headphones, get behind your set, and go. Thousands of drummers have done it that way. Practicing rudiments, either on a real drum or on something less noisy, can be a lot more fun if you do that to music too.

Record yourself
It's hard to really listen to yourself while you're playing. That's why many musicians record their practice sessions. A Walkman with a built-in microphone is basically all you need, but you'll get more enjoyable and instructive recordings if you use better equipment, such as a minidisc recorder with a separate microphone, or any other more or less professional type of home-recording equipment.

And finally
Two great ways to learn how to play? One, play as much as you can. Alone, or in a band. Two, go out to see other musicians play. Living legends or local amateurs, every gig's a learning experience.

4. BUYING DRUMS

You can get yourself a new five-piece drum set with cymbals and a throne for as little as five or six hundred dollars. Want to start out even cheaper? Then buy secondhand, or just get a snare drum or a practice pad and a pair of sticks. This chapter tells you what you should know before you go out shopping. What to pay attention to once you're in the store you'll find in Chapters 5 and beyond.

A brand new five-piece drum set may cost anywhere between about four hundred and four thousand dollars, or even more. What's in between those extremes?

For gigging
A decent drum set and a decent set of cymbals, good enough to be played at a proper gig, will set you back somewhere between a thousand and fifteen hundred dollars. From that point on, things can only get better – and more expensive.

Comparing prices
When comparing drum set prices, take a good look at what you're going to get for your money. The cheapest sets often come with cymbals, but most are offered without. Similarly, the more you pay, the less (!) chance there is that hardware will be included. Drum sets without hardware are usually referred to as *shell sets* – which, in turn, may come with or without a snare drum.

Hardware
A basic hardware set usually has bass drum and hi-hat

pedals, a snare stand, and a straight cymbal stand. Sometimes a second (boom) stand is included, too, or even a throne. Some manufacturers offer pre-packed hardware sets. Prices start at about two hundred dollars.

Better
The differences between a decent starter's set and top-of-the-range professional equipment have become harder and harder to spot in recent years. So why spend extra money on an expensive set?

A 'richer' sound
A more expensive set should produce a 'more expensive' sound – a 'richer' sound, you might say, with punchier lows and brighter highs, more color and carrying power. These results derive from the features that come with a higher price: selected woods for the shells, better workmanship, more research & development, original designs rather than copies, and hardware that's sturdier, easier to adjust, and better looking. And of course, if you're really prepared to fork out a lot of money, part of what you pay will be for status, too.

More to choose from
Paying more also usually means there are more colors and drum sizes to choose from. Low-budget series are often only available in two or three colors (usually red, white and black), and in the basic five-piece setup – so you can't add matching toms later on.

The heads
One technique used by manufacturers to keep the price of entry-level sets down is to use inexpensive, low-quality heads, which won't allow the drums to sound as good as they can. Fortunately, it won't cost you too much to replace them with a set of good, professional batter heads (see Chapter 7).

CYMBALS
You can get yourself a ride, a crash, and a pair of hi-hat cymbals for as little as a hundred fifty dollars – but don't expect them to sound very pleasing. If you want

professional cymbals, be prepared to pay ten times that amount or more. A set of intermediate cymbals, good enough to get you through a proper gig, will set you back some five hundred dollars.

Nothing you can do
There's a vital difference between drums and cymbals: pretty much every drum set can be made to sound at least decent, with some good heads and some good tuning. If a cheap cymbal sounds cheap, however, there's nothing you can do about it.

The other way around
A tip: Shop around for cymbals first, and see how much that leaves you for a drum set. Yes, most people do it the other way around, but just remember that low-budget cymbals are more likely to offend your ears than low-budget drums ever will.

HEADS AND STICKS
How often you have to change heads and how long it takes to break a stick largely depends on how hard you play, but also on the sound you're after. If you happen to like the crisp sound of a new snare drum batter head, you'll have to replace it long before it has worn out.

An hour or a year
Some heavy-hitting pro drummers replace the batter heads of their snare drums every night, and the batter heads of their tom toms every third night. There are also pro drummers who use the same batter heads for over a year. And sticks? Some drummers (definitely not just pros) go through three pairs a night, while others use the same pair for months.

In between
If you play, say, six to eight hours a week and you don't play really loud, the batter heads on your toms and bass drum may last six months or more before they start losing their sound. Snare drum batters go quicker, after perhaps one or two months. Resonant heads can stay on much longer. If you're not an aggressive drummer, a pair of sticks

will last you at least a month, unless you keep time on the edge of your hi-hats.

Some prices
A pair of pro-quality sticks generally costs around seven to ten bucks. A professional 14" drum head will set you back about ten to fifteen dollars, and most 22" heads sell for around twenty to forty dollars.

SECONDHAND
For a used instrument in mint condition you can expect to pay about half of what it would cost new. Age is not usually the most critical factor in determining the price of secondhand musical instruments. Indeed, sought-after vintage instruments may well sell for similar prices to comparable new ones.

Cymbals
You'll come across plenty of secondhand ride cymbals and hi-hats, whereas crashes and other cymbals are quite rare. Why? Rides and hi-hats hardly ever crack, unlike thinner cymbals such as crashes and splashes. Also, drummers tend to want to replace their rides and hi-hats with cymbals that have different timbres sooner than they replace their crashes.

Privately or from a store?
Used instruments can be found in music stores, but also in pawn shops or advertised in newspapers and music journals, on the Internet, and on bulletin boards in music schools and stores. Purchasing a used instrument from a private individual may be cheaper than buying the same instrument at a store.

Questions
One of the advantages of buying a used instrument in a shop, though, is that you can go back if something turns out not to work properly, or if you have questions. Another difference is that a good dealer will not usually ask an outrageous price, but a private seller might, either because he doesn't know any better, or because he thinks you don't…

CHAPTER 4

WHAT ELSE?

Of course it doesn't hurt to read everything you can find before going out to buy an instrument. But you might end up with just as good an instrument if you simply go into a music store, fall in love with the first set you lay your eyes on, decide that it loves you back as soon as you start playing it, and buy it right away. The instrument you buy should make you feel good. In the end, that counts more than the exact number of plies or the type of wood that has been used. The audience won't notice the technical details of your instrument, but everyone will know whether or not you're having a good time.

Guideline

Most well-known drummers have one or more endorsements: They play a certain brand of instruments, and the company uses their name for advertising. Such ads can be a good guideline if you're buying stuff. On the other hand, buying the instrument your favorite drummer plays won't make you sound like him or her. It won't even make you play better – unless it makes you feel better.

The music store

A store with an enormous number of instruments on display may be confusing, but a big selection allows for more direct comparisons. On the other hand, a smaller store may help you focus on the details. So if there are various stores in your area, you may want to visit them all. Listen to a variety of instruments – and listen to a variety of salespeople as well; each has his or her own 'sound' too.

Try it out

In a good store you'll be allowed to play-test the instruments. Some stores even have sound-proofed rooms for the purpose. Good stores also have knowledgeable staff who really like their jobs. Good service is important too. For example, can you come back if you have further questions, and will they help you tune the drums they sold you?

Another drummer

Whether you're buying new or secondhand, it's a good idea to bring another drummer along. After all, two people see and hear more than one. Having an experienced drummer with you may also reduce the risk of passing up an excellent instrument that needs some repair work – or a lesser-known brand with very strong attributes. Besides, it's easier to judge the sound of an instrument if you have someone else play it so you can listen from a distance.

Buying online
You can also buy musical instruments online or by mail-order. This makes it impossible to compare instruments, of course, but most online and mail-order companies offer a return service for most or all of their products: If you're not happy with it, you can return it within a certain period of time. Of course the instrument should be in new condition when you send it back.

Catalogs, magazines, Internet
If you want to know all there is to know, then read every instrument review you can find in drummers' and musicians' magazines. Also, stock up with brochures and catalogs. A word of warning, though: Besides having a wealth of information to offer, literature from manufacturers is designed to make you want to spend a lot more than you have, or have in mind – so ask for a price list too. The Internet is a good source for up-to-date product information too. You can find more about these resources beginning on page 128.

Fairs and conventions
If a music trade fair or a music convention is being held in your area, check it out. Besides finding a considerable number of instruments that you can try out and compare, you will meet plenty of product specialists, as well as numerous fellow drummers, who are always a source of information and inspiration.

TIPBOOK DRUMS

5. GOOD DRUMS

What a drum sounds like depends on many things, ranging from the shell's material to its diameter, depth and thickness, and to the hoops and the lugs. This chapter tells you all there is to look out for when buying a set of drums or a single drum. Hardware follows in Chapter 6, heads and sticks in Chapter 7, and cymbals in Chapter 8.

The shell is the basis of any drum. The material, its dimensions, and the way it has been worked can tell you a lot about why a drum sounds the way it does. So that's where this chapter starts, followed by some basic information on different types of lugs and hoops. Specific things to look for in snare drums, bass follow on page 34.

Maple and birch

Most bass drums and toms have wooden shells, and so do many snare drums. For professional drums, maple is the most popular type of wood, followed by birch. Many pages and hours have been filled with discussions on the differences in sound between the two – which suggests that those differences aren't really that big.

Blindfold tests

Some drummers say maple sounds warmer, some say birch does. Some find birch more percussive, others will tell you the same about maple. Characteristics such as a wide tuning range have been ascribed to both types of wood as well. Many experts seem to agree that maple makes for a mellower sound and a longer sustain than birch, yet others stress its 'explosive nature'. Some brands promote birch drums as 'recording drums' but major recording artists use their own birch drums on stage too, and even more drummers play maple both live and in the studio. And yes, most drummers fail in blindfold tests when trying to tell whether it's a maple or a birch drum set they're listening to. The moral of this story: Go for the drums, don't go for the wood.

Harder and brighter
Other types of wood used include eucalyptus, mahogany and Australian hardwoods. Generally speaking, the harder the wood is, the brighter and more focused or more articulate the tone of the drum will be.

Not specified
The type of wood on budget drums is usually not specified. As they are made of softer woods (*i.e.*, Filipino mahogany, basswood or lauan), these drums will usually produce a sound that's often characterized as warm, fat, or round.

Outer and inner plies
Lower mid-range drums may come with one or two plies of maple or birch. An outer ply does more for the looks than for the sound. A hard inner ply can enhance projection, brightness, and definition, and thus improve the sound.

Metal and other materials
Metal shells are used most often for snare drums. Remo is the inventor and sole user of Acousticon, a wood-fiber material of variable hardness, which is used for drum set shells as well as for percussion instruments. Some companies use other materials, such as carbon fiber or Plexiglas. Being hard, they generally give a louder, brighter sound.

Shell sizes
The two main shell sizes are diameter and depth. The wider a drum is, the lower it can be tuned. The deeper it is, the deeper its sound will be. So a 10x12 tom sounds deeper than a tom in the traditional standard size of 8x12. Today, most drum sets come with these deeper toms, usually known as *power toms*.

Thinner and thicker
Most professional drums have relatively thin shells, measuring around 3/16" or 4/16" (4.5–6.5 mm). It takes good wood and craftsmanship to build shells that thin. That's one of the reasons why most lower-range drums have thicker shells, often in the 5/16"–6/16" range (8–9.5 mm). Thinner drums tend to speak more easily and produce a more open, transparent sound, while thicker drums sound more focused or tight.

Plies
Shells are often made up of six or nine thin plies of wood. For mid- and higher-range shells, the exact number of plies is usually specified. A little theory: Adding extra plies, and so making a shell thicker, stresses the high frequencies in the sound, while you may lose some bottom end. More plies in a shell of the same thickness will make the sound a touch drier or tighter and less responsive. Conversely, a *solid shell*, consisting of a single ply only, makes for a very responsive drum.

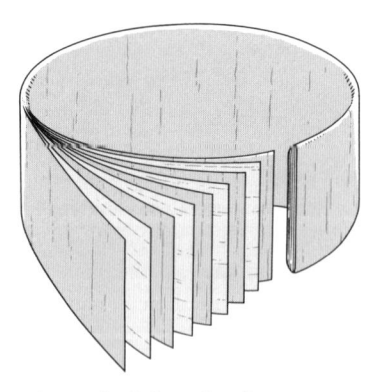

Drum shells are often made of six or nine plies.

Alternative shell construction
A few small companies (Brady, Tamburo, Le Soprano, Troyan) use staves to build shells, in a fashion similar to the construction of wooden congas or casks. Usually, but not always, such shells are considerably thicker than plywood shells.

The bearing edges
The *bearing edges* of a drum 'bear' the heads. Their exact

shape – they are generally angled at 45° – has a noticeable influence on the sound. A sharper edge makes for a 'sharper', brighter sound; rounder edges make for a 'rounder', mellower, less articulate sound. Sharp edges are found on more expensive drums only, not least because it takes longer to make them. No matter what shape they are, bearing edges should always be level and even.

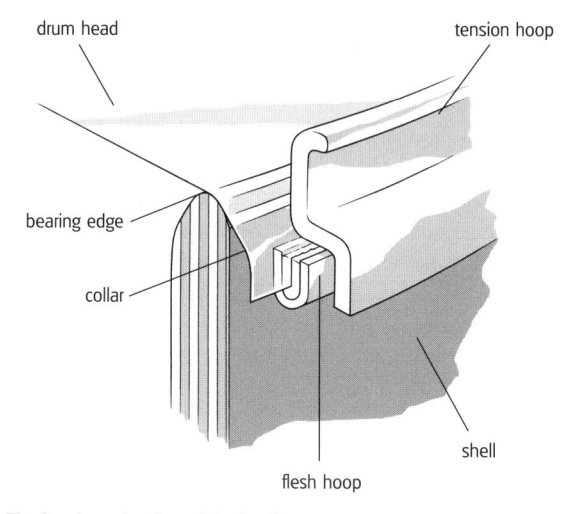

The bearing edge 'bears' the head.

Reinforcement hoops

Some drums have two extra wooden rings on the inside, close to the bearing edges. In the old days they acted as reinforcement rings, keeping the shell from losing its round shape. Nowadays these rings, with a width of about

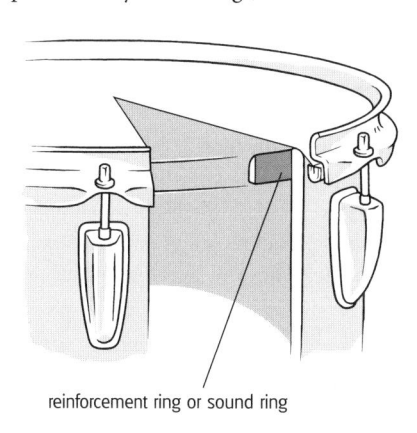

1", are largely used to help determine the sound – so they often come with names like *sound rings* or *sound focus rings*. The fact that they increase the shell thickness at the edges is supposed to slightly stress the attack and the higher frequencies.

Covered drums
Most lower priced drums come with a plastic covering, which withstands scratches, bumps and most other minor knocks a lot better than lacquer ever will. Check to see that the covering fits nice and snug all around the shell. The seam should ideally be held under one pair of lugs.

Lacquer and wax
Non-covered drums are usually finished with high-gloss solid or transparent lacquers. As an alternative, they may be stained, or – rarely – treated with wax or oil, which gives a matte look. The finish on more expensive drums generally consists of a larger number of coats, which makes it look better and last longer.

ROUND AND LEVEL
The shell largely determines the quality of sound in a drum by allowing the heads to vibrate as freely as possible. In order to do so, shells should be round and level. If they're not, the drum may be hard or even impossible to tune. Also, drum shells should be slightly undersized. The following checks are more worthwhile performing on older sets than on new ones.

Undersized? Check
Almost all shells are slightly narrower than the indicated size of the head. This 'floating head design' allows the head to vibrate freely. Simply look at the shell from the side, and see if there's a small, even gap between the shell and the *flesh hoop* of the head. If there's no such gap, the drum's sound may be restricted. It's mainly low-budget covered drums that suffer from this problem.

Bearing edge? Check   Tipcode DRUMS-003
Remove the heads and take a close look at the bearing edges, and trace them lightly with a fingertip. If they aren't

perfectly even, you may get buzzing sounds when playing the drum. A bit of very careful sanding may help, for instance if the unevenness turns out to be nothing more than a bit of spilled lacquer. Avoid drums with dented edges.

Round? Check **Tipcode DRUMS-004**
If the width of the gap between the shell and the flesh hoop varies, then either the shell or the flesh hoop isn't as round as it should be. Try replacing the head. Measuring the shell diameter at opposing lugs may show that the drum is not perfectly round – but it's hard to judge this well without some experience and good tools.

Level? Check
To see if a shell is level, you need a perfectly level surface. Most tabletops won't do. Take the heads off, put the shell on the surface, insert a light and check to see if there's light shining from under the edge. If you don't trust the flatness of the surface, slowly rotate the drum and see what happens in various positions.

HOOPS AND LUGS
Even hoops and lugs contribute to a drum's sound. Both come in various designs.

Pressed hoops
The majority of drums come with *pressed hoops*, made of steel. Mighty Hoops, Power Hoops and Super Hoops are some of the trade names for pressed hoops that are slightly heavier (usually around $^3/_{16}$" or 2.3 mm thick). They may add a bit to the attack and make the sound a bit 'heavier' and drier. Also, their increased thickness helps prevent warping.

Die-cast hoops
Die-cast hoops don't warp at all. You mainly find these very heavy hoops on more expensive snare drums, which is where they're considered to be most effective, adding extra solidity, weight and definition to rim shots and stick shots. Some companies have die-cast hoops on their toms too, often in more expensive series only.

CHAPTER 5

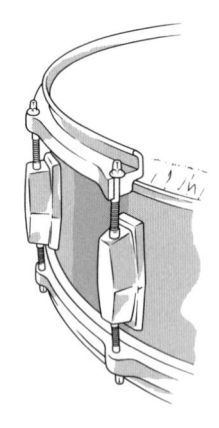

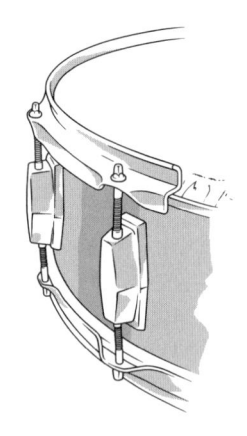

Die-cast hoop (left) and pressed hoops look very different.

Drums with tube lugs, long lugs, and small lugs.

Wood

Most bass drums have wooden hoops. Less expensive ones often come with synthetic or metal hoops (see page 38). Wooden hoops can be found on some expensive snare drums too, and there are a few sets available that even have wooden hoops on the toms. On these drums, wooden hoops help produce a very warm, 'woody' sound.

Lugs

Drums can often be recognized by their lugs, which come in all kinds of shapes and sizes. Most new drums have small lugs, known as *single lugs*; there's one row of lugs for each head, each lug receiving a single tension bolt. Up until the mid-1990s, many drums had *long lugs* or *double lugs*, which receive a tension bolt at either end. These lugs are also known as *flush bracing* or *high-tension lugs* – even though the very moderate tension on the average drum head does not really justify the latter name.

Fashion and taste
The choice between single and double lugs depends on fashion and taste more than anything else, and the same goes for variations such as the tiny *low-mass lug* or the 'classic' *tube lug*, the latter being no more than a tube with threaded ends. Some companies make all their series, from entry-level to top of the line, look similar by using the same lugs all over; other companies do the opposite, giving every series a unique look.

Self-aligning
The *self-aligning nuts* in most lugs help prevent you from damaging the thread of both nuts and tension rods, and they also adjust to slightly different hoop sizes. These nuts are kept in place by plastic inserts, which sometimes double as anti-detune devices by exerting slight pressure on the tension rods.

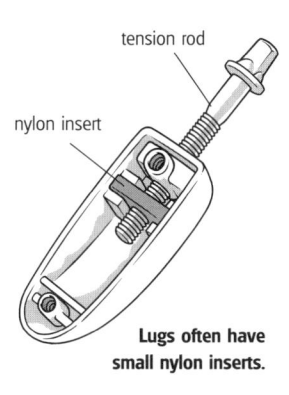

Lugs often have small nylon inserts.

How many?
Most 22" bass drums and 14" snares have ten lugs for each head. Toms up to 13" usually have six, and larger toms come with eight. Cheaper sets may have fewer lugs, which doesn't affect the ease of tuning or the tuning stability as much as you might think. Drums with too few lugs are usually toy instruments.

A coarser sound
Some high-end snare drums have eight lugs per head too – not to cut costs but to produce a sound that may be described as coarser or more open. Some brands use five lugs on 10" toms. This doesn't harm the sound or the tuning stability, but it may take some getting used to when tuning.

Gaskets
Small gaskets underneath the lugs are sometimes advertised

as sound enhancing items, but their main task is to prevent the lugs from damaging the wooden exterior of the shell. Most covered drums come without such gaskets.

Plating and coating
Traditionally, all hardware is chrome plated. Chrome is more durable and less susceptible to scratching than any other finish. Gold plating is softer than chrome plating. Solid brass is what it sounds like: solid brass.

THE SNARE DRUM
The snare drum is the most personal drum of your set; that's why professional touring drummers who don't bring their own sets will still often take their own snare drums. It also explains why many drummers have more than one snare drum, so they can pick a specific sound for a specific style, mood, or sound – a shallow one with a tight sound for funky stuff, a deep one for major backbeats.

Replace
In an entry-level set, the snare is most often the one drum that doesn't match the quality of the rest of the set. Drummers often replace it with a better one as soon as their budget permits.

Material
Snare drums come in a dazzling variety of shell materials, sizes and configurations. Compared to wood, metal shells sound brighter and project better. Most metal snares have steel shells. Brass and bronze are generally said to sound slightly mellower. Wood shell snare drums tend to produce a warmer, fatter sound.

Sizing it up
The best-selling snare drum sizes range from 5x14 to 6.5x14. The deeper the shell, the deeper the sound. For a really meaty, beefy sound you could try a 8x14, though drums this size are quite rare. Smaller, high-pitched snares are mainly used as add-ons, often positioned to the left of the hi-hat. *Piccolos* are most popular for that purpose, ranging in size from 3x13 up to 4x14. Smaller snare drums, with 12" or 10" heads, come with non-standardized names

like *soprano* and *sopranino*. Again, depth is a major factor. A 7x12 drum, for example, will produce a rather deep, yet high-pitched sound.

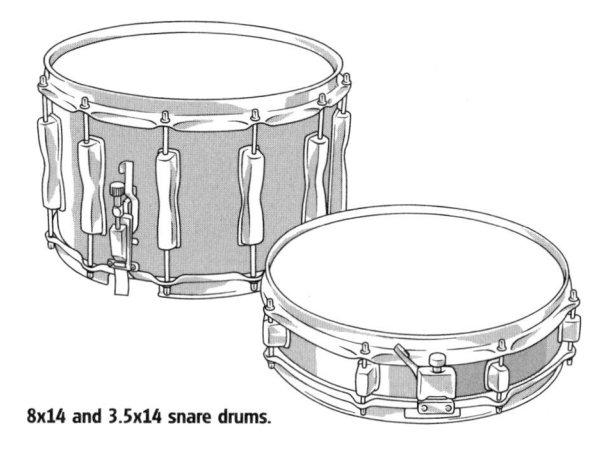

8x14 and 3.5x14 snare drums.

Snare strainer

Most snare strainers are quite straightforward *throw-off* affairs, and that's basically all you need. They shouldn't rattle in the 'off' position, and they're supposed to operate quietly and easily, without any need to hold the drum with your other hand to keep it from falling over.

Tension

Good strainers allow you to adjust snare tension with the snares on the head. If so, adjust the tension while tapping the head, so you can hear what's going on. Knobs on both the strainer and the butt end make it easier to center the snares. There's more on this in Chapter 8, *Tuning and muffling*.

Strings or straps

The snares are attached with either strings or straps. Strings are more likely to break, but both can (and will) last for years. A tip: When trying out snare drums, always check that the snares are centered, with either end an equal distance from the edge. To find out whether the tension on the snares is the same left and right, gently compare the tension on the outer snares. Really gently: If you accidentally overstretch a strand, it will rattle, unless you cut it away.

Snare bed

For a non-buzzing, tight and crisp sound, the snares should also touch the bottom head over their entire length. Snare drum shells have been modeled for this purpose. When looking along the snares, you'll see that the shell is a bit shallower where the strings or straps run over the edges. Because of this so-called *snare bed* the snare-side head surface is slightly concave, allowing for optimal head-to-snare contact.

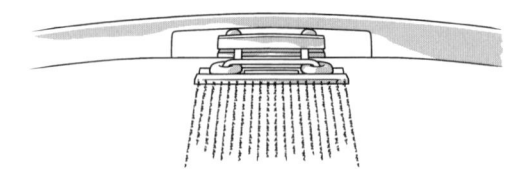

The snare bed: the shell is a little shallower where the strings run over the edges.

Over the edge

Parallel action strainers are quite complicated snare systems that keep the snares under tension while in the 'off' position. These strainers, which allow for very precise snare adjustment, used to be very popular for some years. Now, they can only be found on a few higher-range snare drums. So-called *semi-parallel* systems that, likewise, made the snares extend over the edges of the drum, have also largely disappeared. One supposed advantage was that the extended snares had a better response.

THE BASS DRUM

The bigger the drum, the lower it will sound. And the longer. For bass drums low is okay, but long isn't. That's why most bass drums are being muffled, making for a rather short, though big, punchy, and solid sound.

Sizing it up

The 16x22 bass drum has been the most popular size for many years. Previously, the best-selling bass drum size was the 14x22. The versatility of the 16x22 allows its use in many different situations, giving plenty of bottom end without losing focus or definition. Traditionally, jazz drummers go for a much smaller bass drum (14x18 or 16x18) with a rather high tuning.

In between, or bigger
The 20" bass drum, producing more low end than an 18" and more focus than a 22", gained popularity when fusion took off. If you like lots of low end you may want to try a 24" or even the rare 26". Bass drum shell depths usually vary from 14" (still known as standard depth) to 18" and sometimes more, the extra inches mainly adding to the depth of the sound.

Kits for kids
A kit with an 18" or even a 16" bass drum can be appropriate for a 'junior' instrument. In the lower price ranges, however, 18" bass drums are hard to find. There are special drum sets for kids too, but they're usually of a lesser quality than the average entry-level instrument.

Tension rods
In the past, bass drums were always tuned using T-rods. By the late 1990s most of these had been replaced by standard key rods, which take up less space on the road and give the drum a cleaner look: It is impossible to tune your bass drum heads very precisely and keep the T-handles in line with the bass drum hoop.

Fast adjustment
However, T-rods do allow for fast adjustment of the bass drum sound – which you may want to do quite often, as bass drums tend to be more dependent on room acoustics than the other drums. Also, often just a few turns on one or two T-rods on the batter side are enough to give a bass

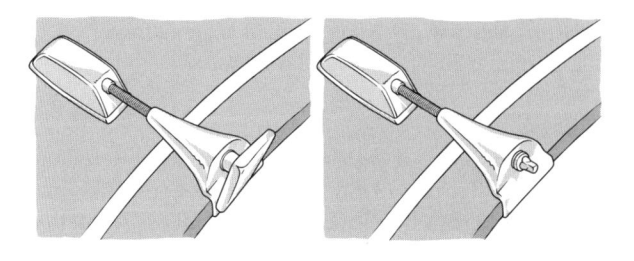

A traditional T-rod and a standard key rod on a bass drum hoop.

drum a fat, dry sound for some songs or a higher, more resonant tuning for others.

Hoops

Most entry-level sets come with hollow metal bass drum hoops, with a small rubber insert to allow proper attachment of the bass drum pedal. Wooden hoops, as found in higher price ranges, add a bit of warmth to the sound of the drum. In between are hoops made of synthetic materials such as ABS. They may not look as good as wood, but they're not as vulnerable and they don't sound that different, really.

Claw hooks

Wooden hoops are easily damaged, if not by bumping things against them, then by the *claw hooks*, which rarely fit the profile of the hoop like a glove. A tip? When replacing bass drum heads, always put the hoops back in their original position, so the claws don't make unnecessary marks on the hoop. Some high-end sets feature die-cast claws hooks, instead of standard pressed ones, and an occasional set comes with felt inlays in the hooks. Plastic hoops don't use claw hooks at all; they have 'built-in' ears, just like tom and snare drum hoops.

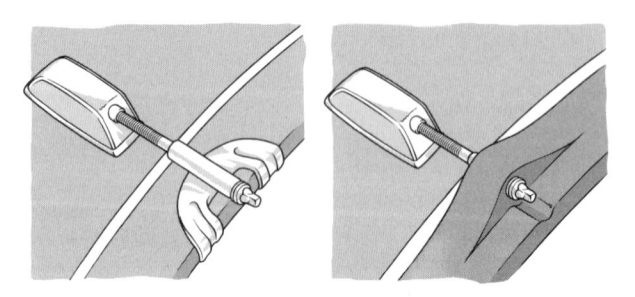

A wooden hoop with claw hooks and a plastic one with 'ears'.

Spurs

Though some spurs may look very impressive, they don't do much more than prevent the bass drum from rolling over or sliding away from you. Most designs offer one preset angle, which is basically all you need. Setting the height of the spurs is something you usually do just once, eliminating the need for all kinds of memory features.

GOOD DRUMS

Spikes
Spurs come with sharp spikes for use on wood or carpets. For other surfaces (and for transportation, if you want to avoid bleeding shins and other damage), you can replace these spikes with rubber tips. Usually this is a matter of twisting the rubber tips up along the threaded end of the spurs. Bayonet catches work even better for this purpose, but they're rare. Less rare, unfortunately, are the designs that require you to pull the rubber tip off with your fingernails. Some floor tom legs come with convertible feet too. As there is no forward motion to stop, these spikes seem to make less sense than the ones on bass drum spurs.

Toms on the bass drum?
On some higher end sets, the rack toms are mounted on separate stands or on a *drum rack*, rather than on the bass drum. Why? Because the bass drum sound is believed to be enhanced by relieving it of the strain of one or two toms resting on it – which is open to discussion if the bass drum is as muffled as it usually is. More important, many high-end bass drums have very thin shells that were not designed to carry the weight of two toms plus a holder. There's more about drum racks on pages 57–58.

TOMS
Rack toms and floor toms are available in an incredibly wide variety of sizes, some series even featuring a choice of three or more shell depths for each diameter.

Rack toms
The most extended drum series offer rack toms from 8" up to 16". The only uneven sizes are 13" and 15". Occasionally, 6" toms are available too.

12" and 13"
The 'standard' drum set, as it has been sold for many years, comes with 12" and 13" rack toms, which are quite close in size, and therefore in pitch. The 16" floor tom that comes with this standard setup is substantially bigger, and lower. If you want actual differences in pitch between your toms, this configuration won't really work. Want to know more? Check out Chapter 8, *Tuning and muffling*.

Fusion and other sizes

As an alternative, many brands offer so-called fusion sets. These have smaller toms, with head sizes two inches apart. Such a set, often consisting of 10", 12", and 14" toms, is much easier to tune to even intervals. In many series, though not the budget ones, you are free to choose your own sizes.

Smaller, not higher

When selecting sizes, pitch is not the only consideration. An example. In a traditional jazz setup, the first tom, a 12", may be tuned considerably higher than a 10" tom from a rock drum set. Apart from a higher pitch, it will have a different sound too, even if both drums are from the same brand and series. The 12" will produce a tighter sound with lots of attack, while the 10" will sound fat, and 'bigger' than it really is.

Five options

Taking a 12" tom as an example, there are many shell depths to choose from. Most semi-pro and pro series offer two choices, entry-level series just one, and only a few series offer all of those listed below.

- The traditional **standard size**, 8x12, is mainly used in jazz and fusion.
- The description **power toms** generally refers to two variations, 11x12 and, more commonly, 10x12; these have been the most popular sizes for years.
- An **in-between size**, 9x12, started to gain popularity in the late 1990s, usually marketed under names that suggest a fast response. (A traditional 8x12, however, will

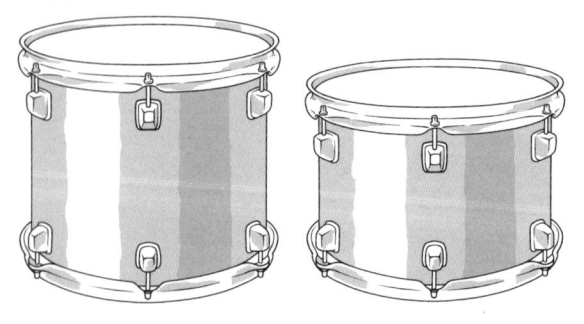

Toms come in a variety of depths: a 10x12 power tom and a standard size, 8x12.

always be even faster). Sets featuring these in-between sizes usually have shallow floor toms (*e.g.*, 13x16).
- The deepest toms have **symmetrical** or **square sizes** (12x12), but these haven't been popular for quite a few years now.
- Then there are drum sets designed for easy transportation, a tight sound, or both, featuring **very shallow** toms (5x12, for example).
- ... and there are also drums that have **no shells** at all, each drum consisting of nothing but a round frame, a tuning system and a head.

Floor toms
The most popular floor tom is the 16x16, followed by the 14x14. Much less common are 18" and 15", but some companies make these sizes too. Floor toms usually have square sizes, though extra deep ones (17x15, 16x14) have been produced as well. Most 18" floor toms are 16" deep. An 18x18 would hardly leave any room between the bottom head and the floor, preventing the sound from developing. The response of a drum that size would be rather sluggish, too.

Feet off the floor
In the late 1980s and early 1990s, many drummers, especially in fusion, replaced their floor toms by slightly shallower drums that were mounted on a stand, increasing the response as well as floor space. The 12x14 and 13x15 are the most popular sizes in what's commonly known as *hanging* or *suspended floor toms*.

TOM HOLDERS
Most drummers mount their rack toms on the bass drum, rather than using separate stands or a drum rack. Many of today's tom holders or *tom mounts* incorporate some kind of isolated mounting system, which prevents the hardware from absorbing most of the sound of the toms.

Tubes and rods
Loads of entry-level sets come with tom holders modeled on a very basic yet effective Pearl design, which consists basically of two sets of two tubes, each with a tilter in the

middle. Another basic design involves one center post and two L-shaped rods for the toms. Contrary to the aforementioned design, these L-rods do not intrude the shells. Most other holders are a combination of these two systems.

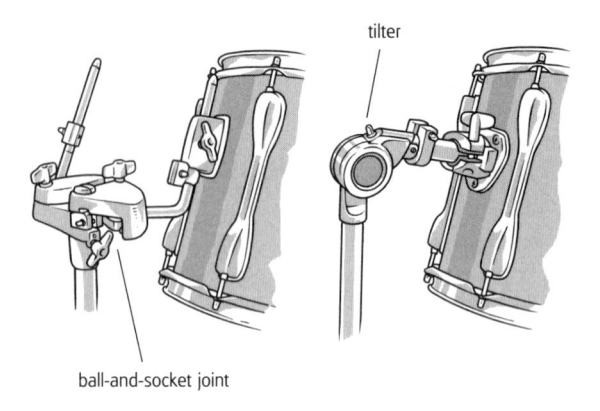

Two different tom holders.

Toothless tilters   Tipcode DRUMS-005

The tilters are most often *ratchet tilters*, which use two sets of interlocking 'teeth'. *Toothless tilters* offer finer and faster adjustment. *Ball-and-socket joints* do so too. One advantage of ball-and-socket joints is that they allow for omni-directional adjustment using just one thumbscrew.

Which one?   Tipcode DRUMS-006

Apart from the ease of adjustment, the actual differences between tom holders aren't that big, and bad ones are hard to find. Tom holders always come with small metal clamps that 'memorize' your settings, allowing you to set up fast, while also adding to the stability. Some trade names, now often used as generic names, are *memory locks*, *key locks* and *stop locks*. These locks are also used on hi-hat pedals, for example. Some tom holders have hexagonal arms, which help stabilize the drums, and some allow you to mount a third holder, next to the ones for the toms.

Disappearing vibrations

If the tom bracket is attached directly to the shell, you may experience a loss of tone and sustain when you mount the drum on its holder. The test: Tune a tom, play it and listen to its sound while holding it by the hoop. Then mount it on the tom holder and listen again. If you hear a difference, the reason is that it's not only the heads that vibrate, the shell does too. If the bracket is attached directly to the shell of the drum, a lot of these vibrations will be absorbed by the mass of the metal of the bracket and the tom holder.

Isolated tom mounting

In the early 1980s drummer Gary Gauger introduced a solution to this problem. In his Resonance Isolation Mounting System (RIMS), the toms are mounted in rubber, hanging from their tension rods. The original tom bracket is attached to a side plate. Many companies have come up with their own solutions, collectively known as *isolated mounting systems*. Others use copies of the original RIMS.

Floor toms

Though floor toms may also benefit from isolated mounting, the effect on rack toms is much larger. Some brands do offer special floor tom legs to allow greater resonance from these drums.

Tom mounted in RIMS.

LISTEN UP

Once you know what you're looking for, it's time to start listening to the drums. Here are some tips.

The same heads

When comparing drums, use the same or similar heads on

them. If not, you're comparing heads more than you are comparing drums, since the heads account for most of the sound. Also make sure the drums have similar tunings. In Chapter 8 you'll find that this involves more than tuning them to roughly the same pitch.

The best heads
If you want to hear what the drums really sound like, it's best to use medium clear heads on the toms and a medium coated head on the snare drum, both without any muffling: Muffling makes drums sound nice and fat, but also very much alike. Please refer to Chapter 7 for examples of the various types of heads.

Isolated mounting
If you compare a drum set with an isolated mounting system to one without this feature, the latter is likely to lose out, even if it's a much more expensive set – but then you're comparing mounting systems rather than drums.

The difference
What does money buy you, in terms of sound? Higher-priced sets offer what's often referred to as a richer sound. There are lots of lows, mids, and highs in the sound, and they're all in balance. This is what makes the instrument speak, as it's sometimes described, and what turns it into a really musical instrument. On a good drum set you will hear each note on each particular drum, even in the fastest rolls you can play, without things getting muddy. Drums that speak well also project well; their sound will cut through, and you're less likely to need amplification when playing in a band.

Timbre
The exact mix between lows, mids and highs determines the instrument's timbre, or the 'color' of its voice – whether it sounds fat, dark, green, bright, transparent, solid, sweet, subdued, yellow, or harsh. This is where it comes to taste, really. There's no such thing as a typical rock drum, a typical jazz drum, a typical studio drum, or whatever. What makes a 'typical' fusion drum set or a 'typical' heavy metal drum set are the sizes, the heads and the tuning – not the drums themselves.

Sustain, attack, response
When testing drums, play them as loudly and as softly as you plan to play them. Listen to the balance between the attack (the initial sound of the stick hitting the head) and the tone (which is what follows). Also listen to how easily the drums respond. If you do quiet gigs too, drums should be able to sound at their fullest even when played softly.

Tuning
Tune the drums the way you plan to play them. If you've got a sensitive ear you can compare tuning ranges as well. How high and how low do the drums go, without losing their tone? You may find that expensive drums are not easier to tune than budget instruments. It's the other way around, actually; it takes more time (and tuning experience) to balance out the wider sound range that high-end drums produce.

Everything
What a drum sounds like is determined by everything that is attached to it, and by every aspect of making it. The number of plies, the shell thickness, the bearing edge, the type of wood, the finish, the hoops, the heads, the lugs... So in the end, after having discussed all details, the only thing you should really listen to is the entire drum set – because that's what you'll end up playing.

Too long
After playing drums for fifteen minutes or half an hour, you'll hardly be able to really listen to all the subtle differences between one instrument and the other anymore. Take a break, or come back the next day. Also, try not to compare too many instruments with one another. Instead, select three snare drums, for example; play them; replace the one you like least – and so on.

SECONDHAND
Pretty much everything that has been said above also goes for used drums and drum sets. Of course there are a few special things to pay attention to when buying used instruments.
- Check if everything is **complete and in working order**.

CHAPTER 5

Are all the hoops, lugs and tension rods present? A used bass drum may have lost its front head and everything that's supposed to come with it.

- Check if the drums **tune properly and easily**. If not, check the heads. Also, the shell and the hoops should be perfectly round and level.
- The condition of the **finish** often indicates how carefully the set has been treated. Check wooden hoops, especially, and see whether the snare drum hasn't scratched the lacquer from the left rack tom.
- Drum sets can live to a **ripe old age**. Twenty or thirty years or more is no problem, provided they have been looked after. Expanding used sets with matching drums may be a problem however, especially – but not only – in the lower price ranges.
- The **brand name on the heads** says nothing about the brand of the drums!
- Older used sets may come with **single-headed toms**, also known as *concert toms*, which have a short, not very resonant sound.
- The lug nuts of older sets may be kept in place by **springs**, rather than by nylon inserts (see page 33). These springs tend to vibrate along with each beat, unless they have been muffled with small pieces of foam plastic, or by encasing every spring in a piece of plastic tubing.
- European drums from the 1960s or earlier may have **metric sizes**. Fitting drum heads can be made to order, but they're expensive.

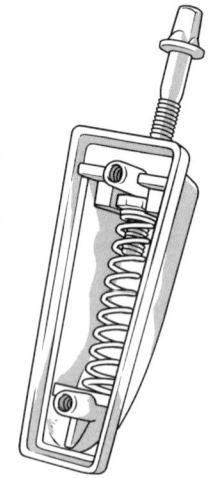

An old-fashioned lug with a spring.

6. HARDWARE

The key requirements for stands, pedals, and all other hardware items are pretty basic: Every piece of hardware should be stable, sturdy, easily adjustable, and noiseless.

If a drum set comes with hardware, check out all the separate items. Some cheaper drum sets come with nice stands but have awkward pedals, for instance, while others offer less quantity (the stands are not as heavy) but more quality (everything works better and pedals move faster). Another tip: If you're not an extremely heavy hitter, you probably won't need extremely heavy, bulky stands.

Hardware sets
If hardware is not included, most brands offer two or three hardware sets which you can choose from, but of course you're free to go for another brand too. However, using accessories and instruments from one brand only may improve the looks of your set, as everything is likely to have the same styling. Tom holders usually come with the drums, so they've been dealt with in Chapter 5.

BASS DRUM PEDALS
A snare drum is your most personal drum, your ride cymbal your most personal cymbal, and your bass drum pedal is your most personal piece of hardware. Good mid-range pedals that can take you through any gig are available for some hundred to hundred twenty-five dollars, but you can also spend much more.

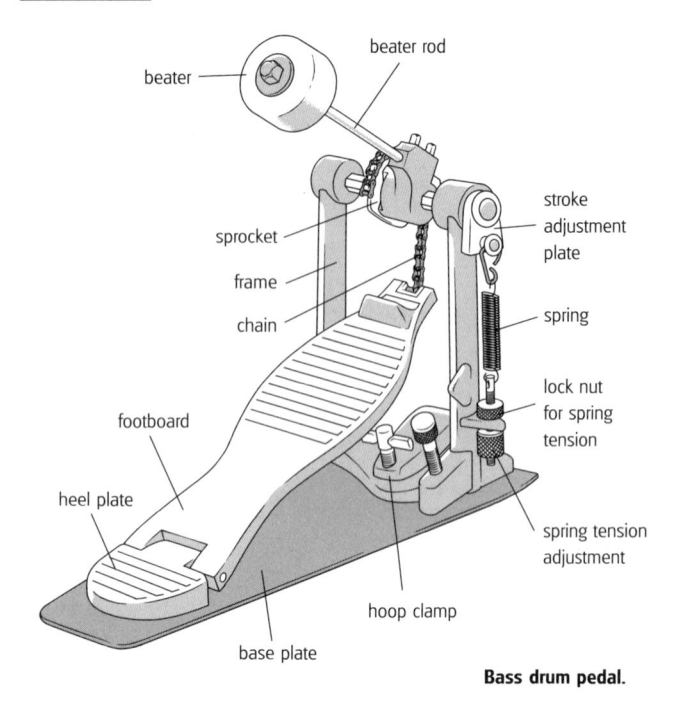

CHAPTER 6

Bass drum pedal.

Spring tension
Tipcode DRUMS-007

Every bass drum pedal comes with an adjustable spring. The higher the tension, the harder you'll have to work to depress the pedal, and the quicker the beater will come back. Usually, drummers with a heavier foot technique use heavier spring tensions and vice versa – and as always, there are numerous exceptions to this rule.

Chain or strap

Pedals basically come in two versions: They're either *chain-driven,* or they employ a fabric strap to drive the beater shaft. These types feel different, and not just because the material is different: The entire assembly is different, too. On most chain-driven pedals, the chain runs over a round sprocket, with the main axle passing through the sprocket's center. This makes for a very even feel or *action.*

Lighter action

Strap-driven pedals, on the other hand, often have what's known as an *eccentric cam*. This results in a lighter action, the footboard traveling a little further. There are also chain-driven pedals with eccentric sprockets, usually providing an action somewhere between the other two types.

Adjustable action

Very few pedals feature an adjustable action, which influences not only the feel of the pedal, but the resulting sound as well. Adjusting it to a heavier feel will usually help produce a heavier sound too, depending on the construction of the pedal and the range of adjustment. Playing around with the settings of such pedals may help you find out whether you like a heavier or a lighter action – and once you decide what you prefer, you may realize you don't need a pedal with an adjustable action at all.

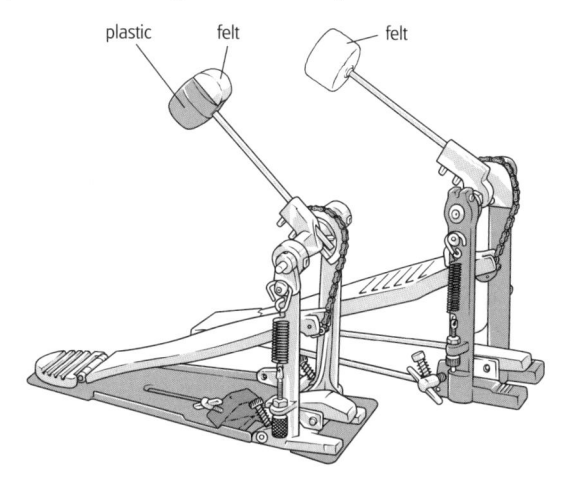

A bass drum pedal with a regular chain drive system (L), and one with an eccentric sprocket. Note the different beaters.

Which one?

A 'heavy' drummer may use a pedal with a relatively light action, and vice versa. Some drummers even use different pedals for different styles of music. One may have a light action when they play *heel up*, pressing the pedal down somewhere in the middle of the footboard, and another with a heavier action when they play *heel down*, with their entire foot on the footboard, using all the leverage the pedal provides – or vice versa…

Lighter action, lighter spring setting?

If a pedal 'feels' too heavy, can't you just lower the spring tension? Yes and no. Yes, because that will make for a lighter feel. And no, because the spring tension also influences the way the beater comes back to you – unlike adjusting the action, for example. Conversely, adjusting the action influences the distance your footboard has to travel. Adjusting the spring tension does not.

Chains and teeth

The sprocket wheel that chain-driven pedals traditionally used to come with, has gradually been replaced by less noisy, felt-lined wheels, either with or without a couple of 'guiding' teeth. If there are any teeth, check that the chain matches them. A double chain adds stability to the pedal. As chains are unlikely to break, life expectancy isn't necessarily increased by making them twice as heavy. Double chains, however, may add stability to the pedal action.

Stability

The more stable a pedal is, the more efficiently your energy will be translated into sound. A *base plate* (also known as *pedal plate* or *stabilizer plate*) will help, and will also reduce unwanted noise. Pedals with base plates take up more room in transportation, and they're a bit hard to attach

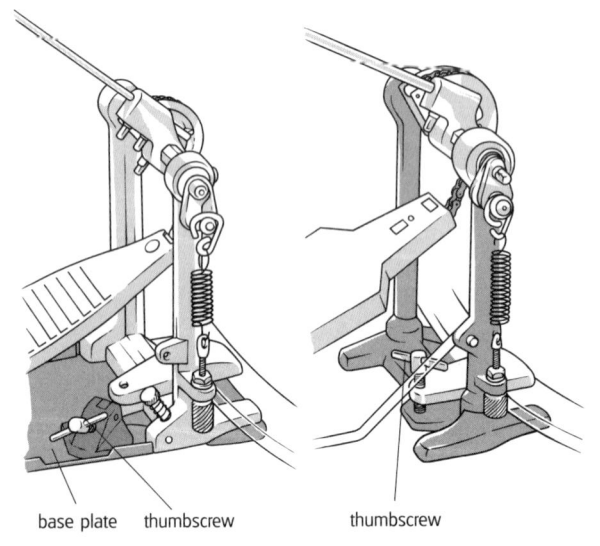

base plate   thumbscrew   thumbscrew

A pedal with a base plate, the thumbscrew mounted to the side of the footboard (left), and one without a base plate, with the thumbscrew under the footboard (right).

to the bass drum if the thumbscrew is situated in its traditional place, under the footboard. On an increasing number of pedals the thumbscrew has been moved to the side, making it easier to attach the pedal to the hoop.

Prime adjustments

The *beater* is usually set at its maximum height, or just a little lower. On bass drum pedals, spring tension is always adjustable. When comparing pedals, set the springs to the same tension. Only a few pedals offer some type of interlocking adjustment screw that really secures this setting.

Beater and footboard angle

The larger the beater angle, the longer the stroke the beater can make, and the louder you can play. Many pedals offer three or four beater angle positions, corresponding to the number of holes in the *stroke adjustment plate* or *spring swivel*. If there's a slot instead of a couple of holes, you can make finer adjustments. When changing this setting, the footboard angle often changes too: If you increase the stroke, the front of the footboard will come up – which may not be what you want. Unfortunately, there are only a few pedals on which both angles can be set independently.

The beater

The beater itself is important for the sound and the feel of the pedal. The harder it is, the clearer or brighter the attack will be, and the more need there is for a protective pad on the bass drum head. Beaters come in felt, plastic, and wood, and some have interchangeable beater surfaces. Felt beaters, the most popular choice, come in different hardnesses. Cheaper beaters are usually on the soft side, producing a mushier sound with less attack. They wear down faster too. Beaters also differ in weight: A heavier beater feels different from a lighter one. If you want to play with a heavier beater there are special weights available which can be attached to the beater rod to speed up the action.

Bearings

A good pedal only moves where it's supposed to move, in the direction it's supposed to move in. Unwanted play or give in the moving parts will absorb at least some of your energy. More importantly, any type of play is bound to get worse. The use of bearings, for instance in the heel joint, prevents play from developing.

Smooth
The action of a bass drum pedal is meant to be smooth and noiseless. The ultimate test? Put it on the counter and move the footboard up and down with your hand. That way you'll hear any noises that shouldn't be there, and you'll easily feel even the slightest irregularities in the action.

Spurs, spikes, or Velcro
To keep them from moving forward, pedals usually have either retractable *spurs* or *spikes*, or a coarse type of Velcro (known as industrial Velcro) or rubber underneath the base plate.

Double pedals
So-called *double bass drum pedals* allow you to use both feet to play the bass drum. When selecting such a pedal, always feel for play in and around the shaft that connects both pedals. Hold the cam or the sprocket of the secondary pedal, and try to move the secondary beater. If there's any play, it's bound to get worse. Very few pedals come with ball bearings in the U-joints of the shaft, although these do prevent play in the long run.

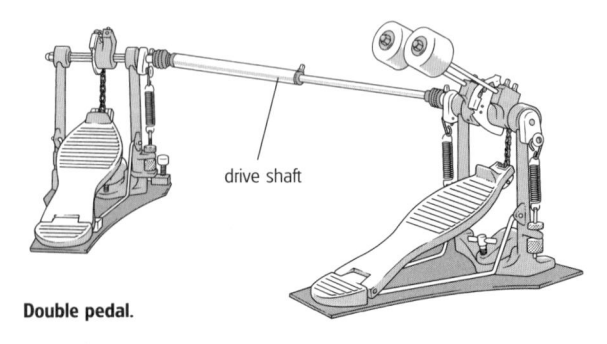

drive shaft

Double pedal.

HI-HAT PEDALS
You judge a hi-hat pedal in much the same way as you would a bass drum pedal. The number of adjustments is much smaller, though.

Spring tension
Tipcode DRUMS-008

Some budget hi-hat pedals come with non-adjustable springs. If the spring tension is too light for the cymbals you're using, the action will be slow. If it's too heavy, you'll have to work too hard. In other words, you're usually better off getting an adjustable one, for which you'll likely pay seventy-five to a hundred dollars or more.

The tilter

When closing your hi-hats cymbals, you may hear a sound something like 'zomp' rather than 'chick'. Usually, this is the result of what's known as *air-lock*, the air between the cymbals acting as a cushion. To prevent this, the bottom cymbal can be tilted. Most tilters use a set screw that slightly tilts a metal washer under the bottom cymbal. Tip: There are also hi-hat cymbals that have been designed to prevent air-lock (see Chapter 8).

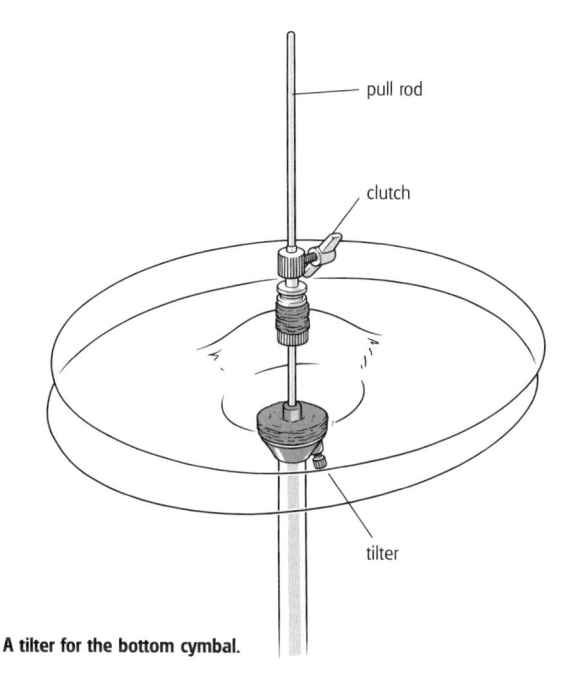

A tilter for the bottom cymbal.

Clutches

The top cymbal is attached to the *pull rod* with a *clutch*. Even the most basic clutches will do in most cases. Some are more expensive because of their looks; others feature a special type of bolt to give them extra grip on the pull rod, or a system preventing the nuts (and eventually the top cymbal) from coming loose.

Felts
The harder the felts that hold the top cymbal, the brighter the sound will be. The same goes for the felt under the bottom cymbal. Some clutches and bottom cymbal holders have rubber alternatives for the old-fashioned felts. The harder the material and the smaller the contact area, the brighter the sound of your cymbals will be.

Drop-lock clutches
A variation on the regular model is the *drop-lock clutch*, allowing you to release the top cymbal by hitting a special handle on the clutch. The top cymbal then drops onto the bottom one so you can play the hi-hat with your sticks while using your hi-hat foot for another pedal, such as the remote pedal of a double bass drum pedal. When you press down the hi-hat pedal once, the drop-lock clutch picks up and 'locks' the top cymbal again.

Locks and spurs
Memory locks are common on the upper tube of the hi-hat stand. Many hi-hats come with one or two spurs, or with Velcro if there's a base plate.

Swivel feet and two-legged hi-hats
A *swivel foot* allows you to swivel the legs around the base of the stand, which gives you additional flexibility in setups with double bass drum pedals, for example. As an alternative, there are hi-hat stands with just two legs, a base plate taking the place of the third one. On some of these pedals, base plate and footboard can be folded up for transportation. If not, they take up a lot of space.

Two-legged hi-hat.

Remote pedals and X-hats

Want an extra pair of hi-hats? You have two options. One is a *remote hi-hat pedal*, which is operated by means of a long cable, so you can position the top section and the cymbals pretty much anywhere you like (somewhere over the first floor tom in most cases). The additional pedal is operated with the same foot as the regular hi-hat pedal (see page 119). Solution number two is an *X-hat* or *closed hat*, which comes without a pedal; it simply holds a pair of cymbals. Setting the tension on the built-in spring makes for tight or loose hi-hat sounds, or anything in between. Using a drop-lock clutch, as described above, your 'closed' hi-hat will always sound a bit loose, as the top cymbal is resting on the bottom one with only the force of its own weight, instead of being pressed against it.

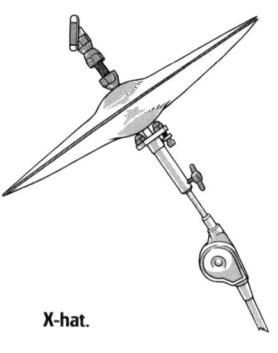

X-hat.

STANDS

Even the most basic stands usually do what they're supposed to do. Still, there are some things to check out. The legs, for example: They're double-braced, on most stands, and you may wonder if you really want to carry the extra weight around, unless you're a heavy hitter.

Fast wing nuts

Some brands have stands with extremely 'fast' thumbscrew/hose clamp combinations; one turn or less is enough to tighten or loosen the clamp. Others take more time. When checking out stands, note that the tubes should telescope easily, and that the legs should easily fold in and out.

Toothless tilters

As on tom holders, toothless tilters on cymbal stands offer infinite adjustment and are faster to work with than the traditional ratchet tilters, which have two sets of interlocking teeth. The finer the teeth, of course, the finer the adjustment. Ball-and-socket joints, as found on some snare stands, can be adjusted in any direction.

CHAPTER 6

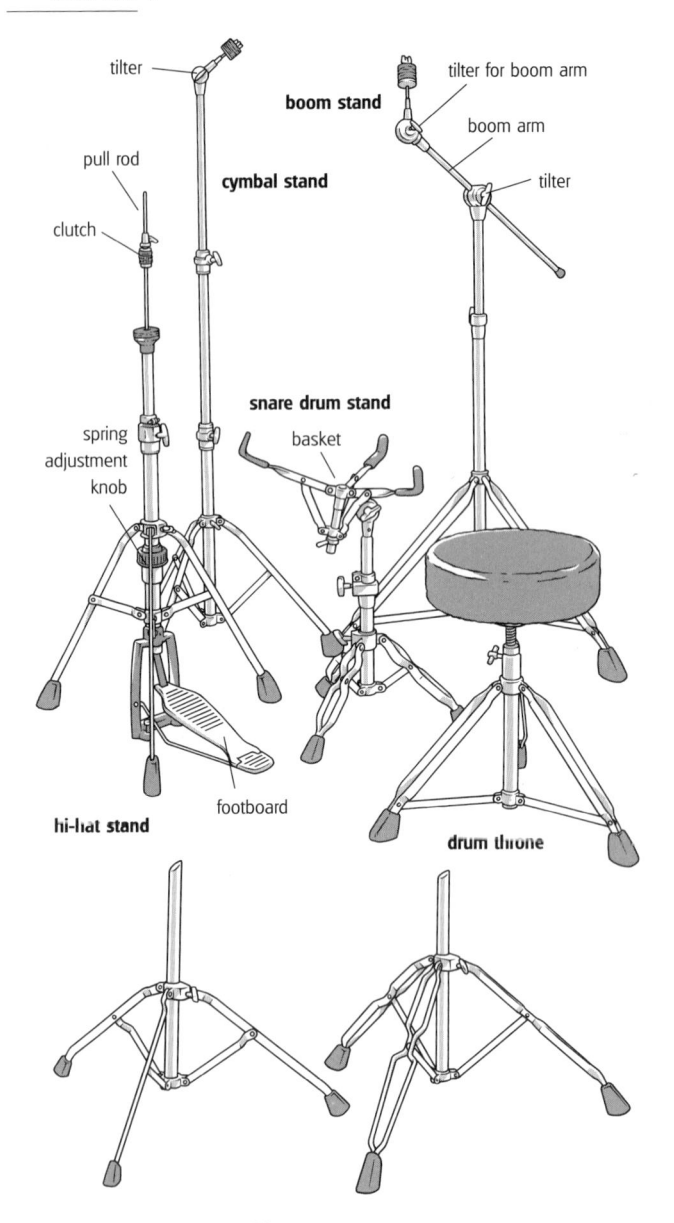

Labels in figure: tilter, boom stand, tilter for boom arm, boom arm, pull rod, cymbal stand, tilter, clutch, snare drum stand, basket, spring adjustment knob, hi-hat stand, footboard, drum throne

Single and double braced legs.

Wing nuts

If the stem of the cymbal tilter has an unthreaded top (known as a *pilot*), that helps preventing wing nuts from falling off when you're tightening or loosening them.

56

Alternatives to the traditional wing nut range from sleeve/nut combinations to clamps and so-called T-tops, all of which save you setup time and prevent you from tightening down cymbals too much (see also page 94).

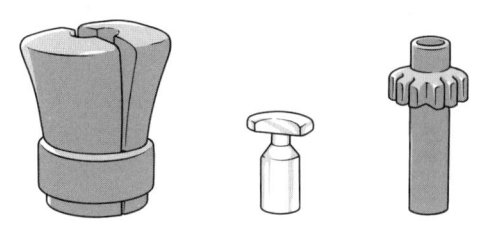

Some alternatives to the traditional wing nut assembly.

Boom stands
Tipcode DRUMS-009

Some boom stands come with counterweights; usually, you can do without this extra mass. If you're in doubt, consider a stand with a detachable counterweight. There are also convertible boom stands: If you don't need the boom arm, you can make it disappear in the upper tube.

Snare drum stands
Tipcode DRUMS-010

The snare drum can be secured between the rubber grips of the basket, and some companies even developed a one-touch handle for this purpose. Tightening the basket too much may stifle the sound of the drum. Most snare drum stands hold 13" drums as easily as 14" ones, and some even take a 15" as easily as a 12". Also consider the maximum and minimum height settings of the stand, especially if it might be used for very deep or very shallow snare drums too.

Two parts

Some cheaper cymbal stands consist of two parts, rather than three. They have one potential drawback only: These parts need to be longer to reach a proper height, so they may not fit a hardware case or bag. Other than that, they can be just fine.

RACKS, CLAMPS AND THRONES

Drum racks help you to set up every item of your set, including microphones, in exactly the same position every

CHAPTER 6

time. They also clean up the look of your set, with a forest of stands making way for three or four sturdy legs. Setting up can be a lot faster too. The bigger your set, the more useful a drum rack will be. For standard five-piece setups and for drummers who like to vary their setup, traditional stands are often more effective than drum racks.

Setup with drum rack.

Multi-clamps

Multi-clamps or *adapters* save floor space. They vary from very basic affairs to clamps with multiple angling possibilities. The ones with hinge joints are the easiest to work with. Some clamps can hold only thicker tubes; others also hold rods.

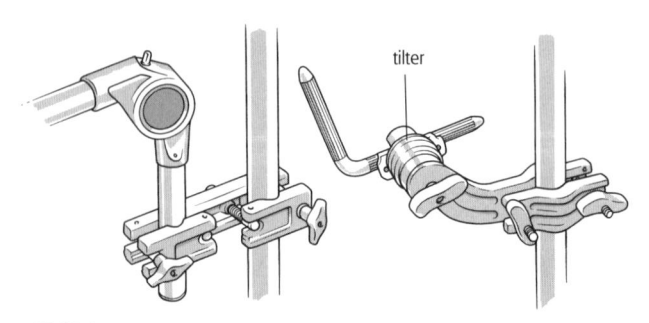

Multi-clamps.

58

HARDWARE

Thrones

If you can't set your throne to the exact height you need, or if it wobbles, chances are your back will tell you something's wrong after a few hours of drumming, after just twenty minutes or, more dangerously, after a couple of months. A good throne easily costs somewhere between seventy-five and hundred fifty dollars. On the most basic ones, the height is set by inserting a bolt into either one of a series of holes in the center tube. If this doesn't allow for the exact height you want, simply drill an extra hole in the tube, or have someone do that for you. Other thrones have threaded rods, which allow for infinite height adjustment. Ideally, turning the seat should not alter its height.

The seat

Traditionally, drum thrones have rather small, round seats. Saddle-shaped seats may offer more comfort, as well as keeping the blood circulation in your upper legs from being cut off. Fabric covered seats, instead of the usual vinyl, help prevent a sweaty feeling. Picking the right seat hardness is largely a matter of taste. A back support (preferably an adjustable one) may be welcome, especially when doing longer gigs.

7. HEADS AND STICKS

Drum heads are the single most important element in the sound you're going to produce, so it's good to take a closer look at what's available. And sticks? The best sticks are the ones you don't even notice when using them.

If you compare a drum set to a home stereo system, the drum heads correspond to the speakers. They are the elements that set the air in motion, and that's essentially what creates the sound that you hear.

The difference
With home stereo systems, it's much easier to hear the difference between two sets of speakers than it is to spot the difference between two amplifiers. Likewise, it is a lot easier to hear the difference between two identical drums with different heads and tunings, than it is to identify two different drums with the same heads and tunings.

The same drums, different sounds
Another example? It's easy to make three identical 12" toms sound completely different, simply by using different heads and tunings. And it's just as easy to make three different 12" toms sound pretty much the same…

Budget heads?
Many budget sets come with budget heads that dent easily, are hard to tune, and don't sound good. Replacing them with professional heads will noticeably clear up the sound. The most audible improvement usually comes from changing the batter heads of the toms, which will set you

back some thirty-five to fifty dollars for the three of them. If you've got the cash, replace the snare drum batter as well, followed by the bass drum batter. It'll all help. For total perfection, replace the resonant heads too.

Medium
The most basic drum head has a clear, single ply of medium-heavy polyester film. This type of head produces an open, even, true sound, with lots of sustain. It's very popular on toms, top and bottom. Some examples: Remo Ambassador, Evans G1, and Aquarian Classic Clear. Medium drum heads basically all have the same thickness, often indicated as 1000 gauge or 1 mil., equaling 0.01" or 0.25 mm.

Medium Coated
The most popular batter head for snare drums is a medium head with a white coating. This coating muffles the head ever so slightly, yet it seems also to produce a somewhat brighter or crisper attack. It also roughens the surface of the head, which is necessary for playing with *brushes* (see page 68). Coated heads are sometimes used on toms and bass drums too.

Two-ply
Heavier players often use two-ply heads, especially on their toms and bass drums. These heads sound fatter, warmer, and shorter than one-ply heads. They also last longer. Some examples are the Remo's Pinstripe, the Evans G2, Aquarian's Performance II, and the Attack Thin-Skin-2. Don't use these heads as bottom heads, because this would kill the drum's projection. A popular combination is a two-ply on top and thin heads on the bottom of the toms. Two-ply heads are usually made up of two 700-gauge plies, which add up to a thickness of 0.36 mm.

Dots
If two-ply heads sound too muffled, you could consider dotted heads, which have an extra piece of drum head material in the middle of the head. These dots affect the sound, making it slightly deeper and more focused, and they strengthen the head at the main point of impact. Dotted heads are mostly used as tom batter heads. Because drum heads with regular dots are difficult to play with

brushes, there are batter snare drum heads that have a dot on the reverse side.

Thin

Thin single-ply heads (700 gauge or 0.18 mm) are used primarily as resonant heads for toms, especially when combined with two-ply batter heads, for better projection and increased brightness. The basic polyester film material is the same as for the other types of heads. It's often referred to as Mylar, which is the trade name of one of the manufacturers (Dupont).

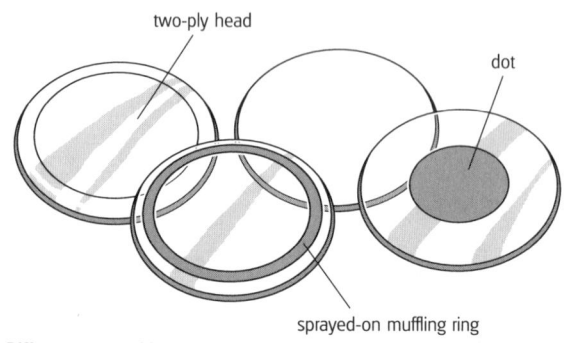

Different types of heads.

Snare-side head

Snare drums need special *snare-side heads*. These heads are extremely thin in order to allow the snares to bounce off the head and create the sound they're there for. Most medium snare-side heads are 300-gauge. Playing very quiet gigs only? Then try a 200-gauge model (only 0.05mm!). Heavy drummer? Go for 500 gauge.

drums	toms batter	toms resonant	snare batter	snare resonant	bass batter	bass front
head types						
transparent medium	●	●			●	●
coated medium	●	●	●		●	●
two-ply/dotted	●				●	●
thin		●				
built-in muffling ring			●		●	●
snare-side head				●		

Different heads and the types of drums with which they can be used.

Muffling rings
Tipcode DRUMS-011

There are various ways to add built-in muffling to drum heads. In the late 1990s the built-in muffling ring became increasingly popular on snare drum (batter) and bass drum heads (both). These very thin rings, which float against the inside of the head, don't alter the attack sound because they bounce off the head when you strike it. The muffling effect comes after the attack, slightly drying out and shortening the sound. Some bass drum heads come with two rings, one of them removable. Sprayed-on muffling rings have only a very slight effect on the sound.

More variations

There are many other types of heads as well. The Evans Hydraulic, for example, includes a touch of muffling oil between its two plies. (Other two-ply heads may look as though they contain oil too. However, the 'oily' colors you see are made by the same refraction of light that makes a rainbow.) Also, there are drum heads with a ridge or a series of tiny holes around the circumference, for muffling purposes; heads which have been made to recreate the warmer, softer feel and the more complex sound of calf skin heads; or extra strong drum heads made of fibers that can be found in bullet proof vests (*i.e.*, Kevlar), and there's lots more.

Two heads, one drum

Finding the right heads is a matter of experimentation, time, and patience. Comparing heads for toms? Take a tom. Put one head on one side, the other one on the other side, and tune them the same. The result will be different from using a head with a proper resonant head, but you will be able to find differences between the two.

Another brand

Changing your drum set may prompt you to change heads too, as some heads sound better than others on some sets. Don't limit yourself. Your toms may sound best with Brand A, while Brand B gets the best out of your bass drum and the ideal combination for your snare is C on top and D down below. Also, similar head types from different brands will behave differently: A two-ply head from one brand may sound a lot warmer or brighter, or it may dent more or less easily than a similar head from another company.

Three more brands
Apart from the drum head brands mentioned above, some drum companies have their own professional drum heads, such as Ludwig, Premier, and Sonor.

STICKS

Drumsticks come in hundreds of different sizes and types. Within all these variations, there are four basic types that every brand can supply you with: the light and slim 7A, the versatile 5A and 5B, and the hefty 2B. Their details are shown in the chart on the next page.

Some basics
Whether you're likely to play with heavier or with lighter sticks depends on a number of things. Generally speaking, heavier drummers use heavier sticks for a heavier sound. Heavier cymbals require heavier sticks to get the bronze to move. Deeper drums need heavier sticks, for pretty much the same reason. However, such sticks are not good for thin cymbals, because they tend to make them crack.

Exceptions
At the same time, there are many exceptions to these rules. While playing softly is harder with heavier sticks, some drummers do so anyway, because they prefer the sound or the feel of a heavier stick. Also, there are drummers who manage to sound surprisingly heavy with surprisingly light sticks. And while most drummers seem to play everything with one and the same type of stick, others use different types for different gigs, different venues, or even for different songs.

For starters
Beginners will find it hard to appreciate the minute differences between the many types of stick available. It may be good to start with one of the standard types – a 5A or a 5B if you like things a little on the heavy side, or a 7A if you have smaller hands. A 2B is generally considered to be a bit too much for beginners. Once you know which

one of these four types suits you best, you can 'fine-tune' your selection by going through the many variations that the many brands offer. Here are some guidelines.

The differences

The best sticks are the ones that make you feel, play and sound the way you like it; they're the sticks you don't even notice when you play. Sticks basically differ in thickness, length, weight, and balance. A thicker stick will feel 'meatier' in your hand, and it produces a meatier sound. The longer a stick is, the easier it goes down (good for playing loud), but the slower it comes up (bad for playing fast). Also, a longer stick provides you with more reach. Of course, both length and thickness influence the weight.

Balance

Balance has to do with weight distribution; a short taper and a thick neck move the weight forward, making the stick feel and sound heavier than it is, and vice versa. Whether a stick has the 'right' balance largely depends on where you hold it and how you play.

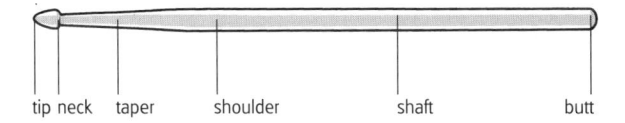

tip neck taper   shoulder   shaft   butt

Not the same

Pretty much every stick maker has its own idea of what the 'standard' 5A, 5B, 7A, and 2B sticks should be. Still, all 5As have something in common, and the same goes for the other standard types. The following chart shows the average dimensions of the four standard types. The same chart works well as a point of reference for any other type of sticks.

type	weight	length	diameter	neck
7A	45 grams	15.75"/40 cm	0.530"/13.5 mm	0.235"/6 mm
5A	50 grams	16"/40.5 cm	0.570"/14.5 mm	0.255"/6.5 mm
5B	55 grams	16"/40.5 cm	0.610"/15.5 mm	0.275"/7 mm
2B	65 grams	16.25"/41 cm	0.640"/16.5 mm	0.295"/7.5 mm

Average dimensions of 'standard' stick models (rounded off).

Feels like more

As you can see, everything increases just a little at a time, yet a 2B feels very (very!) different from a 7A – which also explains the astounding number of models available. Sometimes 'Rock' and 'Jazz' are regarded as standard models too, but the variations in their specifications from one brand to another are much bigger than those in the four standard types listed; the Rock type sold by one brand may be as much as 1.5 times heavier than the next brand's Rock stick.

Hickory, maple, oak

Weight, feel, and sound are also influenced by the type of wood. Most sticks are made of hickory, a flexible yet strong type of wood. Maple sticks weigh less and have a lighter sound. You like the feel, but not the weight of a thick stick? Try a similar model in maple. You like the weight of a stick, bit it's too thin? Again, try a similar model in maple. Heavy player? Try oak. It's heavy, dense and strong, with a bright sound.

The tip

The *bead* or *tip* of a stick is important for the sound; that goes for its material as well as its shape. Most sticks come with wooden tips. Nylon tips, a popular alternative, last much longer and sound brighter. Most stick manufacturers offer distinctive shapes for nylon and wood tips on their otherwise identical models.

Tip shape and size

Bigger tips make for a bigger sound by generating more highs and lows. Small tips yield a very controlled sound, but drum heads dent faster with these kinds of tips. Oval

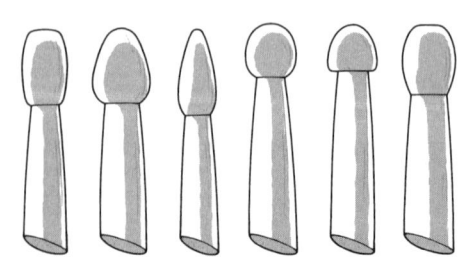

Every tip gives a different sound.

tips offer the largest range of sound variations on your ride cymbal: Changing the angle at which you play the ride changes the sound.

Feels different

Most sticks have a lacquer or a wax finish. How these coatings feel is very personal, depending largely on your type of sweat and skin. A stick that becomes slippery in your hands may feel great in the hands of another drummer. There are also differences between various types of lacquers, of course.

Get a grip

Slippery sticks? You can try a similar stick with a different coating, try playing with drummers' gloves, or wrap some commercially available stick tape around your sticks. Some alternatives are unfinished sticks, sticks with knurled grips, sticks with built-in rubber grips, sticks with thicker grip areas, and so on.

Equal weight, equal sound

Most drummers look for a pair of sticks that are equal in weight and sound. However, the art of matching sticks still lies mainly in trying them out, one by one and two by two. Some brands offer computer-selected pairs that are matched extremely well – but even then you may still want to select a few pairs that all have similar weights and sounds.

Checks

Checking for straightness? Roll the sticks over the counter. Checking for sound? Play them one by one on a wooden counter or tabletop, or use one stick to play the other. Some drummers play their heads – the one on their shoulders – to find sticks that produce the same pitches…

Weight differences

Not many drum stores have a postal scale, though such a device speeds up the process if you want to select a larger number of sticks of similar weights. A basic rule of thumb: If you can't feel the weight difference in the store, you probably won't feel it when you play. 'Identical' sticks, whether pre-packed or not, easily vary 10% or more in weight – and that you can feel.

Non-wood

There is a limited selection of non-wood sticks available, in a variety of materials. Some say that they last longer and are more consistent than wooden sticks, while sounding as good and feeling about the same. Some actually do come very close. Their prices vary between roughly fifteen and thirty dollars.

Wire brushes

Drummers play with more than just sticks. *Wire brushes*, for instance, are mainly used by jazz drummers. The most common type has a rubber grip, retractable steel wires, and a loop end that allows for a variety of sounds, especially on cymbals. Wire brushes, usually just called *brushes*, differ in the exact gauge of wire (a heavier gauge producing a heavier, broader, coarser sound), in the wire material (steel has a more refined sound than nylon), and in the material of the handle (rubber, wood, plastic), as well as in balance and weight. Rubber is the all-time favorite handle material, even though in most cases it becomes pretty sticky after a while. This may vary from one brand to another.

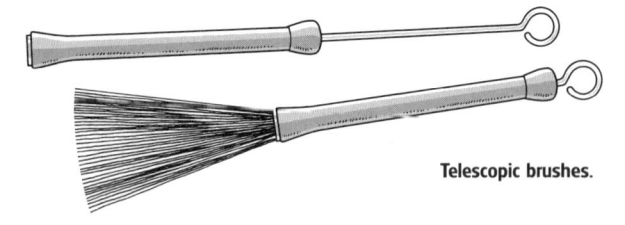

Telescopic brushes.

Multi-rods

You can also use tightly bundled wooden or plastic dowels, commonly known as *multi-rods*. They produce sounds somewhere between sticks and brushes. Multi-rods come in many varieties, with more or fewer dowels, heavier or lighter dowels, and so on. On some types, the sound can be influenced by moving a plastic collar up or down the

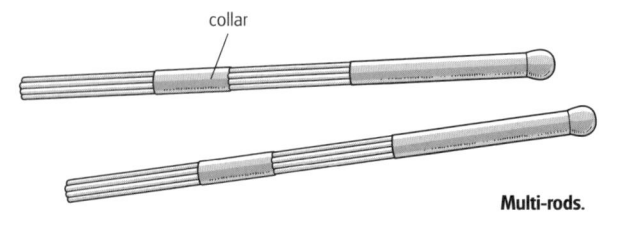

Multi-rods.

dowels. A tip: Most types will sound good only if you don't play too softly.

Mallets

Just like sticks, *mallets* come in loads of different types. Tympani mallets, for instance, with big, soft heads, work wonderfully for long rolls on cymbals.

Brands

Some of the established manufacturers in this area are Agner, Pro-Mark, Johnny Rabb, Regal Tip, Rimshot, Vater, Vic Firth, and Zildjian, every one of them producing dozens of different models, and in some cases different brands as well. This also explains why you may come across two identical sticks with different brand names.

8. CYMBALS

Cymbals look very simple, but they're not. A good cymbal is in fact very hard to make. That's why the better cymbals can cost a lot of money.

Finding the cymbals you like is easier if you know a little about why they sound the way they do. If you plan to use your ears only, skip to the tips on page 76.

Series
Most manufacturers make cymbals in various price ranges, like drums, but they also make series of cymbals arranged by sound characteristics, or series that are aimed at certain styles of music. Cymbal catalogs may give you good information on what to expect from a certain series.

Sounding names
Many cymbals have names that may help you in making a first selection. Power, Full, Dark, and Fast speak for themselves, more or less. Weight indications, such as Medium, aren't as straightforward as they sound: If you compare ten 16" Medium crash cymbals of various brands and series, you'll hear ten quite different cymbals.

Heavier, larger, higher
Many elements influence the sound of a cymbal. Four of them are easy to discern: weight, diameter, profile, and cup size.
- If you had two similar cymbals, one slightly **heavier** than the other, the latter would sound both higher and longer. It would also have a slower response; in other

words, a heavy crash needs a heavy blow to really crash.
- A **larger** cymbal has a lower pitch and a longer sustain than a similar but smaller cymbal. The larger cymbal also needs more power to be able to respond.
- **Cup size** influences volume, response, and the amount of overtones, which make the sound richer. A larger cup makes a cymbal respond faster and produce a louder, more full-bodied sound.
- A cymbal with a **higher bow** will have a higher pitch and a slower response than the same cymbal with a flatter profile.

Interrelated

All these parameters are strongly interrelated – for instance, a heavier cymbal may sound lower than a lighter one of the same size because it has a lower profile.

Hammer marks

The way a cymbal has been worked also has an effect on the sound. The hammering, for instance: The more regular the pattern of hammer marks (the dents on the surface of the cymbal), the more 'regular' and the cleaner the sound will be. An irregular pattern, such as created when hammering a cymbal by hand, helps produce a darker and more complex, 'irregular' sound.

Grooves   Tipcode DRUMS-012

The circular grooves that most cymbals have enhance the spread of the sound. Cymbals that have no grooves (*unlathed cymbals*; see Chapter 13) have a tighter, drier, more compact, more metallic sound. Even, regular grooves promote an even, 'regular', clean sound. Uneven grooves enhance the complex character of many hand-made cymbals.

Alloys

As a cymbal consists of one part only (the cymbal itself), the material plays a major role in determining the sound. Five basic alloys are used in cymbal production:
- Budget cymbals are often made of **brass** or **nickel-silver**, the first producing a warmer sound than the second.
- The oldest alloy is a bronze containing 20% tin and 80% copper. This metal, known as **B20**, is used for professional

series by Zildjian, Sabian, UFIP, and the Turkish cymbal companies.
- The lower tin content of **B8** gives this bronze alloy a slightly reddish tint. Its somewhat tighter sound can be heard in cymbals such as the classic Paiste 2002s, in most professional Meinl cymbals, and in many lower and mid-range series of other brands.
- Paiste's own **Sound Alloy** is closer to B20 than to B8.

'Identical' cymbals

Two cymbals of the same series, type, and size may sound a lot more different than they look. These variations between 'identical' cymbals are generally bigger where B20 is used, and more specifically in cymbals that feature an irregular hammering pattern. In other words, even if you're sold on one particular type of cymbal, listen to and compare several examples of that cymbal before deciding which one to buy.

Budget cymbals

Cymbals often come in pre-packed sets, especially but not exclusively in lower price ranges. If you want to be sure that you'll enjoy your purchase for a long time, unpack the set, and play-test each cymbal.

There are major sound differences between low-budget series too, so you may very well enjoy the ride cymbal from one brand or series and the crash from another. Buying separate cymbals will be more expensive, though, even within the same series.

RIDE CYMBALS

The attack sound of a ride, the *ping*, may vary from a very penetrating, clean sound to something rather dark, thick, and dry. Generally speaking, louder music demands a more definite ping (more definition, that is), which you'll get best from a heavier cymbal. A good test is to crash the cymbal and then play a ride beat at the volume you intend to use the cymbal. If you hear the individual beats from the very start, you're on the right track. Listen to the sound of the ping, which may range from high to low, dry to wet, thick to thin, solid to delicate, mean to friendly, or modest to provocative.

The cup

The cup has a very tight, pronounced sound, but it shouldn't sound as if you are playing a different cymbal when compared with the sound you get from the rest of the cymbal. Also listen to what the rest of the cymbal does, when playing the cup. Does it start to sound along with the cup right away, or is it only the cup that you hear, no matter how hard you play it?

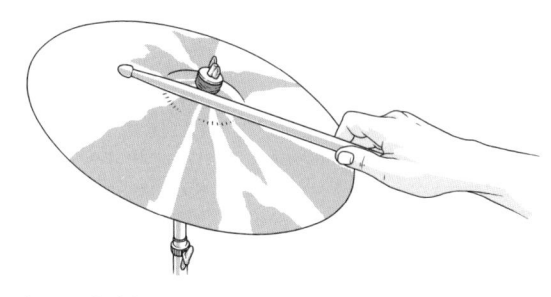

... the sound of the cup...

Crash-ride

Many 18" and bigger cymbals can be used for riding and crashing, and dedicated *crash-ride cymbals* are also available. Such cymbals can be a solution if you can afford only one cymbal.

Professional crash-ride cymbals are rare. Many jazz and fusion drummers use their cymbals for riding as well as for crashing, choosing relatively thin cymbals with an irregular hammering, which produce a wide array of overtones or *harmonics*, as well as having sufficient definition to be used for ride patterns. These cymbals are usually not marketed as crash-ride cymbals, however.

Ride sizes

Most drummers use 20" or 22" ride cymbals, but you can get them in 18", 19", and 21" as well. Smaller and bigger rides are rare.

HI-HAT CYMBALS

When checking out hi-hat cymbals, play them in every way you're going to use them. Depressing the pedal should produce a good, definite *chick* sound. If it's followed by a sweeping tone, don't buy the cymbals. Playing them in closed position should produce a nice, tight sound. If they sound hollow, forget them. Open the hi-hats and play them with sticks, and see how fast they respond. Testing and comparing hi-hat cymbals is easiest if you have a few clutches at hand, so you can switch cymbals quickly and compare. Better still, use a couple of hi-hat stands, one for each pair of cymbals you're comparing.

Heavy bottom
If you need your hi-hats to produce a very definite chick sound, go for pairs that have a considerably much heavier bottom cymbal. Loud drummers use both heavy top and bottom cymbals. Don't hesitate to mix tops and bottoms from various pairs, if the store owner allows you to do so. Cymbal fanatics may even end up mixing cymbals from different types, series, or brands – if the store owner will let them do that.

Air-lock
To prevent air-lock (see page 53), some brands make bottom cymbals with corrugated edges or some extra holes.

Hi-hat sizes
Most drummers use 14" hi-hats; others go for 13". Smaller sets, typically 10" and 12", are mainly used as additional hi-hats on an X-hat (see page 55) or a remote hi-hat (see pages 55 and 124). Larger hi-hats are rare.

CRASH CYMBALS
Some drummers like crashes that cut through everything. Others prefer them to disappear right after the attack, and some want them to sound like a hot shower. The most important thing is that a crash cymbal should immediately produce most of its lows and highs when you play it as softly as you will onstage.

Store versus stage
In the store, crashes always seem to sound longer than they will onstage. The louder the music you play, the larger this difference will be. A crash cymbal that seems to sound forever in the store, will sound a lot shorter onstage.

Too thin
Drummers with a heavy attack sometimes tend to buy crashes that are too thin for the music they play, because in the store thinner crashes sound more pleasant than the power crashes they need.

Different
At a distance, when used in a band, crashes tend to start sounding much more alike than they do in the store. So go for extremes in contrast, but make sure the cymbals you play sound as a set as well.

Crash sizes
Apart from 16" and 18" crashes, the most popular choices in any style, there are crashes in even and uneven sizes from 12" up to 22".

EFFECT CYMBALS
There's a wide range of so-called effect cymbals, such as Chinas and splashes, as well as a host of other variations.

Splashes
Splashes are small, very fast crashes, with sizes from 6" to 12". Heavier splashes will not splash unless they're hit extremely hard. Really thin ones respond real fast – and if you play them real hard, they'll break real fast too.

Chinas and China types
Chinese cymbals were originally made to scare the enemy, and they still tend to scare fellow musicians who come too close. The upturned edge is one of the reasons for their aggressive, rough and exotic type of sound. The Western variations on this theme, with a regular (so-called Turkish) cup often sound mellower, or less 'dirty' than the very affordable, but also more vulnerable cymbals from China.

And more...
Flat rides, which produce a delicate, very controlled ride sound, have no cup at all. *Sizzle cymbals*, which, as their name suggests, make a sizzling sound, have two or more *rivets*, usually near the edge. Then there are special cymbals

CHAPTER 8

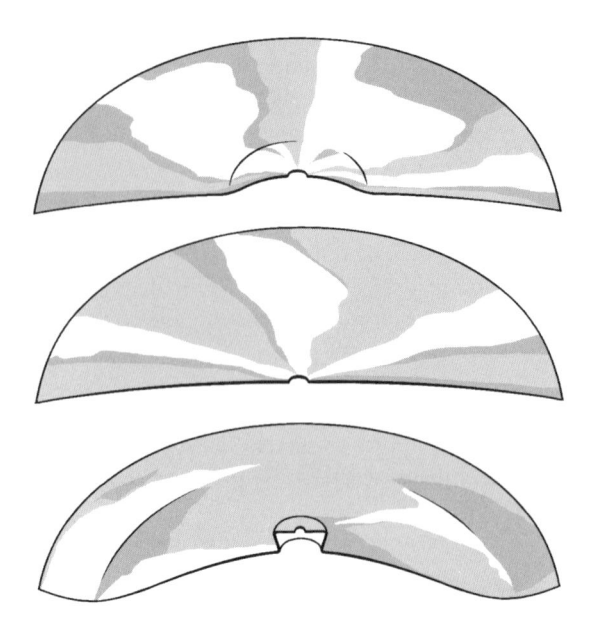

The profiles of a regular cymbal, a flat ride and an original Chinese cymbal.

for percussionists, cymbals that are no more than a big cup, China splashes, cymbals with holes, cymbals with square cups, cymbals with jingles, and much more.

LISTEN UP

- If you're a first-time buyer, start by picking a **ride or the hi-hats**, depending on what you use most for time-keeping. Crashes, splashes, and effect cymbals come later.
- If you're about to replace or add cymbals, **take the cymbals you already have with you**, so you can hear whether the new ones 'fit in'. A tip: Cymbal setups can include as many brands or series as cymbals.
- When play-testing cymbals, use **your own sticks** or a similar pair.
- When comparing cymbals, never listen to more than **three cymbals at a time**. Replace the one you like least with a similar cymbal. Listen. Replace the one you like least. And so on.
- If possible, listen to your final selection **as part of a drum set**, so you can use them the way you do when you play.

- Bring **another drummer** along. Have him or her play so you can listen at a distance, and vice versa.
- No other drummer around? Close the **one ear** that's in the general direction of the cymbals, and play them; this will give you some idea of what the cymbals sound like 'live', in a band setting.
- **The ultimate test**? Use the cymbal in your band. Most shopkeepers won't let you, though, for obvious reasons.

Secondhand cymbals

There are plenty of used ride and hi-hat cymbals for sale. After all, they hardly ever break, they're quite expensive, and many drummers tend to go for a change from time to time. A few tips.

- **Cracked cymbals** will invariably crack further. Don't buy them.
- Check secondhand cymbals for **invisible cracks**. Play the edge of the cymbal with your finger, hold the cymbal close to your ear and listen for the slightest buzzing or rattling.
- Avoid cymbals with a **worn-out hole** (known as a *key hole*); they have been played without a cymbal sleeve (see page 94).
- Cymbals that **shine very brightly** around the hole have probably been mounted too tight, which increases the risk of cracking.
- And other than that: Please enjoy your used cymbals, as much as if you'd bought them new. They can last for **decades**. Splashes, too. Some drummers even prefer old cymbals (especially the famous and rare old Ks from the formerly Turkish Zildjian factory). They're so popular, in fact, that most brands offer special series to recreate the cymbal sounds of the 1950s and 1960s, with names like Traditional, Original, Classic or Nostalgia.

A cymbal with a worn-out key hole.

TIPBOOK DRUMS

9. TUNING AND MUFFLING

Unlike most instruments, drums can't sound out of tune. So why tune them? To make sure they sound as good as they can, and to make sure they sound the way you want them to. It takes seconds to make a great drum sound like a box. It takes a bit longer to tune it to its best. The basics are set out in this chapter, which also includes tips on muffling.

It's up to you how you want to tune your drums – high and tight, low and fat, or anywhere in between. Every drum has a certain range it can be tuned to. Tuning it higher will make it choke, tuning it too low kills the tone. Every drum can also be tuned to a point, somewhere in between these extremes, at which each element of the instrument seems to come together. When you reach it, you'll hear the longest, fullest, biggest, and most musical tone that drum is capable of producing. A tip in advance: Learning to tune drums takes time, so be patient.

One per string
Tuning a guitar is quite easy. For each string there's one tuning mechanism. Each string can be tuned either too low (*flat*), too high (*sharp*), or just right.

Five or more per head
Tuning drums is quite a bit harder, as there are five to ten tension rods for each head. Properly tuning a head means creating an even tension at each rod. What makes things take really long is that adjusting one rod also influences the tension at the other rods.

TUNING AND MUFFLING

The drum and the set

Tuning a drum set requires not only that each head has an even tension all around, making it in tune with itself, but also that there's a balance between the top and bottom heads of each drum. Finally, tuning a drum set also includes tuning the drums relative to each other, creating the intervals (tonal distances from drum to drum) that you like.

12", 13", 16"

The sizes of the drums dictate these intervals to some extent. So if you have a set with 12", 13" and 16" toms, there will be a large interval between the 13" and the 16". Trying to make it smaller by tuning the 13" quite low and the 16" quite high will result in two drums that do not sound like they're parts of the same instrument: The smaller drum will have a fat sound, while the bigger one will sound thinnish.

Drum keys   Tipcode DRUMS-013

Pretty much every brand has its own model of *drum key*, but every key fits every drum. Drum keys are usually provided with a small hole so you can attach them to a key chain. Apart from regular drum keys, there are various types of key that help you tune or remove heads faster, such as speed keys and ratchet keys.

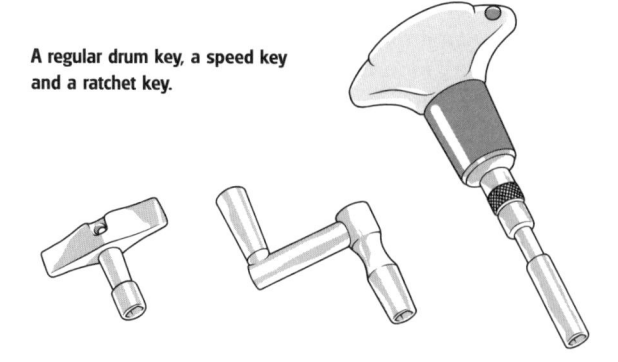

A regular drum key, a speed key and a ratchet key.

BASIC TUNING   Tipcode DRUMS-014

To get most from this section, take a 12" or a 13" tom, as they're easier to handle than a floor tom, and easier to tune than most 10" toms. Remove the heads, which you can do even faster if you use two drum keys simultaneously. Put the drum on a folded towel or a piece of foam plastic so you don't damage the bearing edge.

Worn-out heads

Replace the heads if they're dented or worn out. You can tell a worn-out head because it's no longer level when you look at it from the side. If so, it has lost most of its elasticity and therefore most of its sound. While the heads are off, you may want to clean the hoops, the inside of the drum, the lugs, and the rods.

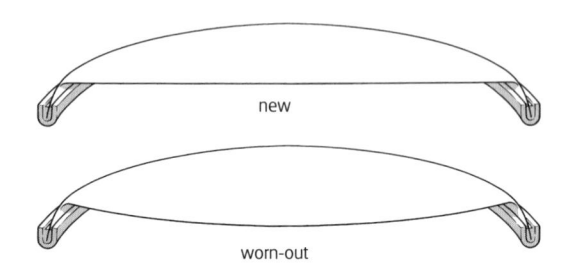

A new and a worn-out drum head.

Basic tension   Tipcode DRUMS-015, DRUMS-016

Put the batter head on the drum. To create a basic even tension all around the head, use your fingers to tighten all the tension rods as well as you can. This may be hard, for instance if your drums have very short tension rods. If so, use a drum key to turn each rod so that the underside of its square head just touches the hoop. In both cases, it helps if you do it two by two, always tightening opposing rods simultaneously. On a drum with six tension rods per head, start with 1 and 2, then 3 and 4, and end with 5 and 6. The lug numbers are shown on the next page.

Higher and higher

Now slowly increase the tension, half a turn per rod at a time, following the illustrated order of lugs or any of the many variations. When the head starts to produce an agreeable tone, you're nearly there.

The pitch

Continue tightening the rods, perhaps in quarter turns

now. Meanwhile, lightly tap the head at each rod, about an inch from the edge, with your drum key, a fingertip, or a stick. As soon as you start hearing the pitch you're looking for, it's time for the hard part: fine-tuning. Fine-tuning is all about making sure the head produces the same pitch all around, at every tension rod.

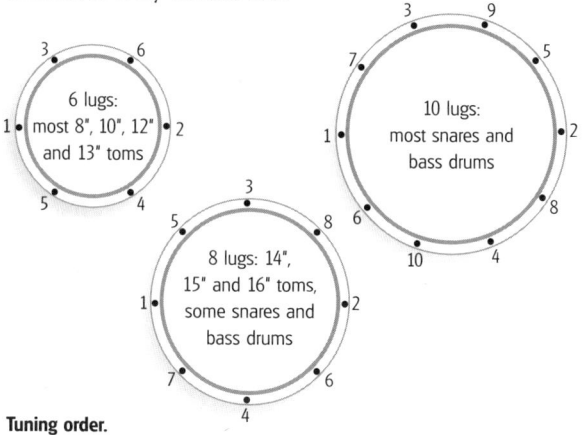

6 lugs: most 8", 10", 12" and 13" toms — order: 1, 2, 3, 4, 5, 6

10 lugs: most snares and bass drums — order: 1, 2, 3, 4, 5, 6, 7, 8, 9, 10

8 lugs: 14", 15" and 16" toms, some snares and bass drums — order: 1, 2, 3, 4, 5, 6, 7, 8

Tuning order.

FINE-TUNING
Tipcode DRUMS-017

No matter how precisely you've tuned this head so far, you'll find that it produces a slightly different pitch at each rod. To even that out and create an even tension and pitch all around takes time. Here's a few tips.

- Defining the pitch is easier if you **place a finger in the exact center** of the head. Just touch it, don't push. Tapping at the lugs will now produce a clearer tone.
- Take as your starting point the one rod at which **you best like the pitch**; this is now lug number 1. The pitch will probably be the same at the opposing lug, which becomes lug number 2.
- **Compare this pitch** to what you hear at lugs 3 and 4. If they sound too low (flat), tighten them a little. Note that the pitch at 1 and 2 goes up when doing this, so loosen them up a tiny bit. Drum tuning is about creating a balance: Give a little here, take a little there…
- Adjust all the key rods until the tension (and the pitch) is even all around. **This sounds easier** than it is. Why?
- An example: the pitch at opposing lugs often sounds identical – but that **doesn't mean the tension is the same** at those lugs. This may be the problem if, for example,

you don't succeed in getting 3 and 4 to sound the same pitch as 1 and 2. If so, try tightening 2 and lowering the tension at 1, or the other way around. If that doesn't work, try the same with 3 and 4.
- When comparing two pairs of rods, also **listen to the pitch at the other rods** from time to time. If the tension at 5 is much too low, on an eight-lug drum, you'll never get 1 and 3 to sound the same.
- If you want to lower the pitch at a certain lug, then don't just release it. **Instead, always tune up**: First, loosen the tension rod until the pitch is clearly too low, then go up from there.
- **Can't manage**? Don't panic. Take the heads off and start all over, either at once, or after taking a break, and consider asking an experienced drummer to help you.

Placing a finger in the middle of the head, tapping, and adjusting the relevant tension rods.

Three options

If your batter head has the pitch you want, mount the bottom head. Basically, you have three tuning options: Tune it to the same pitch as the batter head, to a higher pitch, or a lower one.

1. Tuning the heads to the same pitch creates a long, clear, clean, and even tone.
2. A higher-sounding bottom head will make for a tone that's brighter and livelier, with increased cut and projection.
3. Tuning your bottom head lower will result in a deeper sound – more of a thud, with reduced sustain. The tighter top head helps the stick rebound and accents the attack.

Tips

The only way to find out what you (or your drums) like best is to try each option. Here are some tips.

- **Don't overdo** the pitch difference between top and bottom heads.
- A different tuning for top and bottom may result in a **pitch bend**, *i.e.*, the pitch changes after the attack.
- Some drummers describe option 2 as a big, fat sound. Others use those words for option 3. Both groups agree that there's a **big difference** between 2 and 3…

Muffle the other head

When fine-tuning a head, always muffle the other one; put the drum on your drum seat, or on a folded towel, for example. Also, when comparing the pitches of batter and bottom head, always muffle the other head. If not, both heads will sound similar, even when they're not tuned the same; their pitches will tend to blend and sound like one.

Mounting the drum

If your drum set doesn't include an isolated mounting system (see pages 42–43), mounting a well-tuned tom on its holder may drastically reduce its sustain, resonance, and tone. There are two solutions.

- You can **fine-tune the drum when mounted**. (First, mount the second rack tom too, as they are bound to influence each other!)
- You can provide your toms with **an isolated mounting system**; they're not that expensive anymore. The first solution is not very musical, as you will find that the tom holder now sort of dictates the tuning of the drum – and that's not what it's meant to do.

Detuning

Drums detune because heads stretch quite a bit, especially when they're new. Detuning also occurs because the tension rods back up. Some drums come with a system to help prevent the latter (see page 33). Using softer, non-metal washers under the tension rods may help a bit, and will also make it easier to tune. Lug-locks are among the commercially available products that help prevent detuning by 'locking' the tension rods.

Press
Pressing a mounted, new head down with your hands helps taking the initial stretch out. If you do, you'll notice that it makes the pitch drop considerably. Some drummers even stand on their bass drum heads for this purpose. It can be done – but be careful.

Actual notes
Some drummers tune their drums to actual notes: for example, the 10" to a G, the 12" to an E, and so on. Want to try this out? Then use a piano or a similar instrument as a point of reference. Electronic tuners easily get confused when confronted with the many frequencies that drums produce; for drummers, ears are a more reliable tool to gauge tuning.

The drum's pitch
Another point of reference to find the right pitch for a drum is the shell itself. First, take off all its lugs and mounts. Then, put your arm inside the shell, and balance the shell on one finger. Now tap it lightly to determine its pitch, using a piano or another keyboard instrument, for example, for reference. Tune the drum to that fundamental pitch. This may help you get close to the point at which the drum sounds its best. You can also try this without taking all the hardware off, since that, after all, is how the drum is used; the hardware influences the pitch of the shell too.

Tuning devices
There are special devices that help you tune by measuring the resistance of the rods or, more effectively, the tension of the heads. The latter are not cheap, easily costing around seventy-five dollars or more, and fine-tuning is still up to you, but they can make basic tuning a lot faster. They also help you establish at which rod the tension is higher or lower – even when the pitch sounds the same. The Tama Tension Watch was the first device of this kind.

Adjusting
Many drummers put the heads on with the logo in the same position (between the same two lugs) as the drum's badge. That way, if you take the head(s) off you'll always put

SNARE DRUMS

Fine-tuning a snare drum is very similar, the major difference being that the heads will be a lot tighter. If not, the sound will be more of a *boosh*, and less of a *crack*.

Ten lugs
Most snares have ten lugs, making it hard to keep track of the tuning order. A tip: Write the numbers of the rods on the drum head, or on a ring cut from an old head.

Snare-side head
The snare-side head is pretty tight as well. Because it is so thin too, it's hard to determine its pitch. A starting point to find the right tension is to put the tip of your left little finger against the top of your left thumb. Now feel how tight the fleshy part below you thumb is – and tune the snare side head so that it feels about the same. A very loose snare-side head will produce a 'loose', broad or thick type of sound. Tightening it will increase clarity and projection, up to a point where it's so tight that it becomes hard to get the snares to respond.

Stick in a stick   Tipcode DRUMS-018
If the snares interfere with your snare-side tuning, make them a bridge by separating them from the head. Simply – and very, very gently – insert a stick under the released snares, from left to right, the ends of the stick resting on the counter hoop.

The snares
Adjusting snare tension is best done in the 'on' position. If you need the drum to sound good at all volume levels, lightly tap the batter head while increasing the tension on the snares. As soon as they stop responding, the sound becoming kind of hollow, back up a little. If you play really loud, you can tighten the snares up a bit more.

Detuning the snare-side head
The snares are supposed to 'snap' when you strike the

drum, and then be quiet right away. If they don't, one solution is to deliberately detune the snare-side head. Loosen the four tension rods at either end of the snares, and tighten the others to compensate. Now play the drum again, and note that it sounds as if you have tightened the snares, so loosen them up a bit. When fine-tuning the snare-side head, the tension should now be highest at 1 and 2, a bit lower at 5–8 and 6–7, and lowest at the other four rods.

The other way around

On some snare drums this trick only works if you do it the other way around: Tighten the rods at either end of the snares, and loosen the others. How much you'll have to change the tension depends on pretty much all the factors involved, so experiment.

Snare buzz

Snares are not supposed to respond when you play a tom or your bass drum, or when the rest of the band comes in – yet they do. Don't worry too much, as the resulting snare buzz is heard mainly by you, the drummer. However, if it gets too loud or distracting, there are a few things you can try.

- If your snares resonate when you play one of your toms, try **adapting the tuning of that tom**. You can change its pitch, or try to keep the pitch the same by loosening the bottom and tightening the top head a little, or the other way around. No luck? Then you may have to change the tuning on your snare drum – or both.

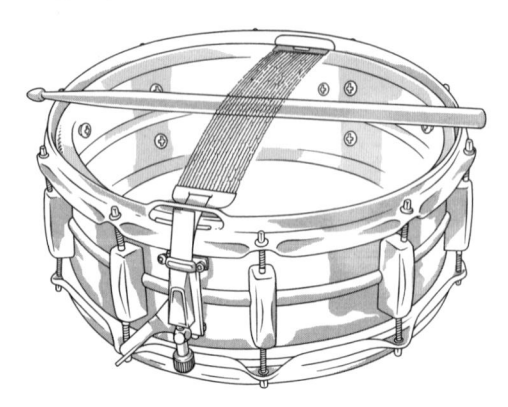

Make a 'bridge' for your snares.

TUNING AND MUFFLING

- **Check the snares.** They're supposed to touch the snare-side head over their entire length. If you doubt their condition, take them off: They should rest flat on a tabletop. If not, replace them.
- The **distance between the snares and the drum's hoop** should be equal on both sides, and the strings or straps should pull evenly, right and left. Contrary to what you might expect, this is not the case on many new snare drums.
- The snare strings **shouldn't be too thick**. Shoelaces are. Your drum store has special snare strings.
- One more option? If someone's playing a solo and you're not doing anything, **release the snares**.

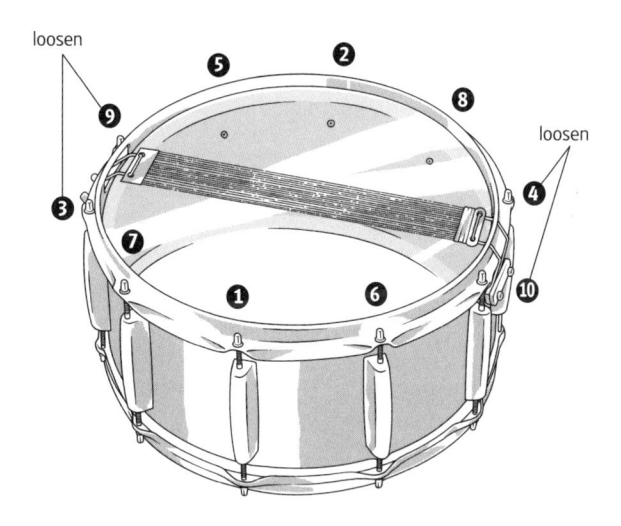

Loosen these four tension rods a little and tighten up the rest to compensate.

Different snares

The exact type of snares also influences your snare drum sound, to a degree. There are snare sets with heavier and lighter strands, with strands made of harder or softer material, with less or more windings per inch, or with less of more strands. The heavier the strands, the more strands or the more windings, the 'thicker' or heavier the snare drum will sound, while strands of a harder metal will make the sound a little brighter. A tip: Not every set of snares will work with every drum. Obviously, an extra-wide set with thirty or even more strands makes no sense on a drum with a relatively narrow snare bed.

The bass drum
Most drummers tune their bass drums really low, often to a point where the heads only just lose their wrinkles. You'll get more of a tone and less attack if you increase the tension, until the point where the drum starts choking again. Really high tunings are mainly used by jazz drummers, on small 18" bass drums.

Interval
As for the interval between the two heads and other tuning principles, bass drums generally behave like toms. Of course, a difference is that most bass drums are muffled, and many have cut-out front heads. A tip: The less muffling you use, the more important it is to apply even tension to both heads.

MUFFLING
For bass drums, tuning and muffling often go hand in hand. Many drummers muffle their snare drums too. Toms are generally allowed to sound wide open.

Muffling the bass drum
There are many ways to reduce the bass drum's tone and ring. Here are some examples.
- For light muffling, check out bass drum heads with **built-in muffling rings** (see page 63).
- A much cheaper alternative is using a **felt strip**, at about one third of the way along the head(s). These strips bounce off of the head at the attack, just like a muffling ring. Felt strips can also be used on the front head only, combined with heavier muffling of the batter head, for example.
- You can buy special **bass drum pillows** that bounce off the head at the moment of impact, allowing for a full-sized attack sound and muffling what comes later.
- A **rolled-up towel**, taped in the angle where head(s) and shell meet, is a lot cheaper. It sounds different too, as it stays in contact with the head.
- The Remo Muff'l is a **polystyrene ring**, held against the

TUNING AND MUFFLING

circumference of the head in a plastic tray. This tray also covers the precious bearing edges of the drum – but it's very effective, especially on batter heads, combined with a resonant head that's only slightly muffled.
- Another old-fashioned yet (cost-)effective muffling method is to partially fill the drum with **shredded newspaper**, or **small pieces of polystyrene**.
- For a really short sound, partially cover the inside of the drum with a **piece of 2" polystyrene**, barely touching the head(s) – or simply put a pillow or a blanket inside the drum.
- If band members complain that your bass drum resonates too much, just **detune one or both heads**. It's fast, effective and very low-budget, and it's also great if you need a tighter sound for just one or two songs.

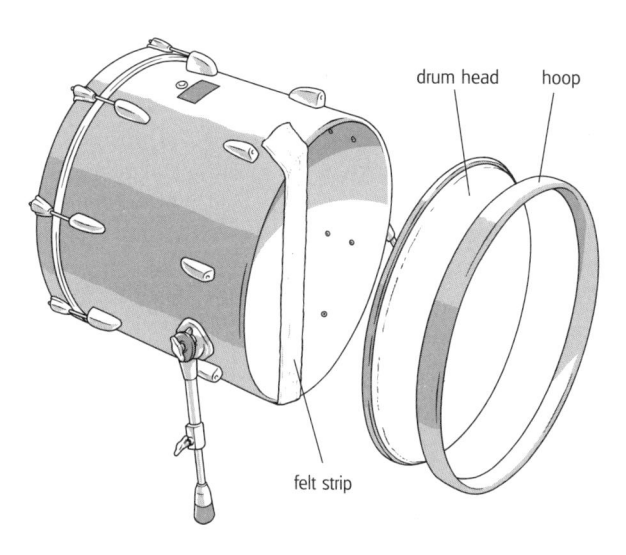

Bass drum with felt strip.

The front head

For a long time, bass drums were played without the resonant front head, effectively reducing resonance as well as sustain. A less drastic solution is to cut a hole in the front head, or buy a pre-cut (*ported*) front head. If the hole is in the middle of the head, opposite the beater, the effect will be similar to having no head at all, even if it's just a small hole: The sound will fly straight out.

Smaller hole
By contrast, a small (4"–6") hole near the edge hardly affects the sound at all. Holes like this are often made so that a microphone can be stuck inside the drum, and they also give access to the inside of the instrument, for instance so that you can adjust the muffling. The general rule: The larger the hole, the more attack and the less tone and resonance. A hole also reduces the rebound of the batter head: the larger the hole, the less rebound.

The entire head
Removing the entire head may result in rattling lug nuts, a deformed bass drum shell, and damaged bearing edges. It's better to cut out most of the head, leaving just two or three inches around the perimeter.

The template and the edge
Many drummers use a cymbal as a template when cutting a hole. However, should your hand slip when you're holding the knife, you'll do less damage if you use a lid or any other flat metal disc instead. There are special templates too, as well as products to cover the sharp edge of the hole. A household alternative is to cut a piece of thin rubber tubing (*i.e.*, gasoline tubing) open lengthwise, and mount it over the edge. Cutting drum heads requires a sharp knife, so make sure to cut nothing but the drum head.

Attack
Increasing the attack sound of a bass drum can also be done by using a hard (wood or plastic) beater, or by sticking a special self-adhesive pad on the point of attack. These pads are made by various drum head and other companies. As hard beaters are more likely to dent the bass drum head, they are often used in combination with bass drum pads – which increases the attack even further.

MUFFLING SNARES AND TOMS
There are various ways to muffle snare drums and toms. Some work for both, others for snare drums only.

O-ring
The O-ring that comes with many snare drums is very

TUNING AND MUFFLING

effective. It mutes the circumference of the head, which is where most (both desirable and undesirable) overtones are generated. You can also buy these rings separately, or carefully cut them yourself, using an old head. The wider the ring, the more marked the effect will be. A head with a built-in O-ring or muffling ring (see page 63) will help produce a more open type of sound, compared to using an O-ring on top of the head. O-rings are rarely used on toms; they muffle the sound too much and they may start buzzing because the heads move such a long way.

An O-ring down-under

A snare drum variation on the O-ring can also be cut out of an old head. Use an old 14" head for a 14" drum, cutting the middle 12 to 13 inches out of the head. Then cut the flesh hoop off. Take the batter head off the drum you want to muffle, place the remaining ring over the bearing edge, put the batter head back on, and tune the drum.

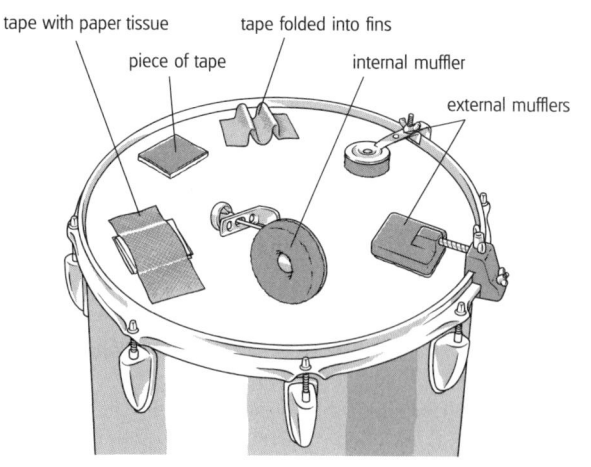

Different mufflers.

Tape

Duct tape (also known as *stage tape*, *gaffer tape* or *cloth tape*) works well on snare drums and toms. It's inexpensive, easy to apply and remove, and very 'experimentable'. Locate the best spot by gently putting your finger on various places on the head while playing the drum at the same time. Folding the tape into fins increases the muffling, and it's even more effective to tape a paper tissue to the head.

The outer edge
Unlike an O-ring, tape and other small muffling devices don't muffle the entire outer edge of the drum, which is where the high, crisp overtones come from. As a result, rim shots and rim clicks will often speak better if you apply a piece of tape. The same goes for other products that muffle the head in small areas only.

Internal and external mufflers　　　　　Tipcode DRUMS-019
Internal mufflers restrict the downward movement of the head, which is very noticeable on toms – so they're hardly used on those anymore. As these mufflers leave the head entirely open, many brush players still like them on snare drums. *External mufflers* are flexible, and fast and easy to work with. They're rare, though; one reason is that they don't move as easily with the head as tape does. They also take up (a little) space in the playing area, and you usually have to take them off for transportation.

Tune, tune, tune
Snare drums and toms are often muffled to reduce the effect of clashing or howling overtones, which are due to badly tuned heads. The better you tune a drum, the less you have to muffle it. More importantly, the more you muffle a drum, the less you'll be able to hear what you paid for!

Miking
If your set it about to be miked, spend extra time tuning it, as microphones easily pick up unwanted overtones. A properly tuned set with an isolated mounting system for the toms is less likely to get its heads covered in tape by a sound engineer who otherwise can't handle the sound of your drums.

Muffling and volume
The only way to muffle your drums so that your neighbors can get some rest is to stuff them with polystyrene, or cover them with rubber discs (see page 14). The types of muffling discussed in this chapter barely reduce the number of decibels you produce.

TIPBOOK DRUMS

10. SETTING UP AND MAINTENANCE

Drummers are among the only musicians who can tailor their instruments to fit them like a glove. This chapter offers some basic tips, and also deals with keeping everything in working order and taking your drums on the road.

If you want to save energy and gain speed and control, the best way to set up your drums is so that you can reach every piece of your instrument without really stretching your arms at any time. The drums in the illustration on page 4 are set up that way.

The throne
As a starting point, adjust the height of your throne so that the tops of your thighs are parallel to the floor. If you're young – and small – this may prevent you from reaching your toms and cymbals. Buying a smaller set (see page 12) helps. A no-budget alternative is to remove the second rack tom, so you can lower your most important cymbal, the ride.

The pedals
Position the pedals so that your shins are angled slightly forwards. Set the length of the spurs of the bass drum so that the bottom of the front hoop is raised one or two inches off the floor.

The snare drum
Have the snare drum at such a height that the batter head is one or two inches higher than your thigh. If you use a *matched grip* (the same grip for both hands on your sticks), tilt the drum towards you slightly. Drummers who play

traditional grip often tilt it to the right, towards the floor tom.

The toms
Set the floor tom at the same height as the snare drum, angled slightly towards it. The rack toms should be angled towards you, again slightly. If the angle is too steep, you'll end up with dented heads: The larger the angle between stick and head, the more easily you'll dent the head. Position the toms so that the lower sides of the batter heads are about four to eight inches higher than your snare and floor tom heads. When set right, they're not so high that you need to raise your arms to play your rack toms, and not so low that you can't play rimshots on them.

The cymbals
Angle the cymbals towards you as well, to make them easier to play and harder to crack. Have the hi-hats about four inches higher then the snare drum, slightly overlapping it. The distance between the two cymbals determines how far your foot has to travel. Loud players often have their hi-hats higher and further apart, and vice versa.

CYMBAL TIPS Tipcode DRUMS-020, DRUMS-021
If you're a heavy drummer and if you use heavy sticks, you should use pretty heavy cymbals, or you're bound to use a lot of cymbals – one after the other. Yet some heavy drummers play pretty thin crashes without ever breaking them. How come? They have good playing technique, for one thing, and they don't try to play *through* the cymbal. Here are a few more tips.
- The stem of the cymbal tilter should always be covered with a **nylon sleeve**, or, as one of many alternatives, a piece of rubber tubing such as gasoline tubing. Without it, you'll create a keyhole in the cymbal, and it may crack from the hole. Also, the cymbal should rest on **a felt or leather washer**.
- Never tighten cymbals down. Crashes and splashes especially should be allowed a generous amount of give, so they can **go with the blow**. Replacing the wing nuts with modern alternatives (see page 57) prevents overtightening cymbals.

SETTING UP AND MAINTENANCE

Cymbal tilter.

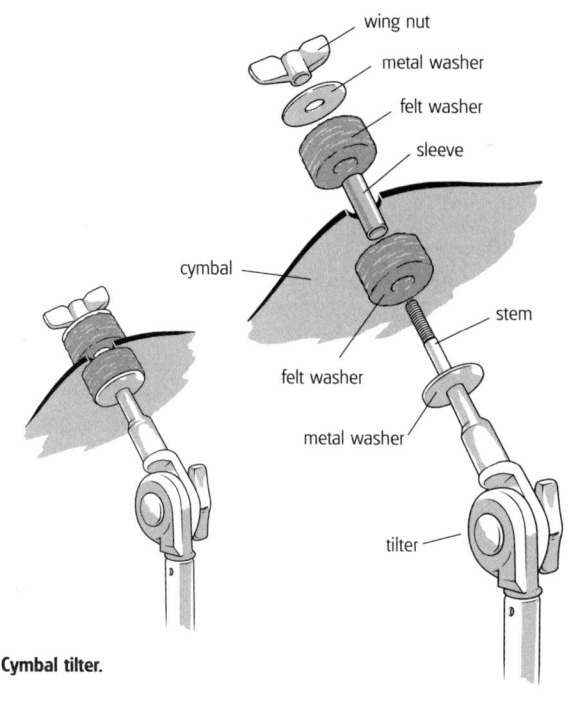

- The **clutch** should be set so that the top cymbal has a little bit of play too. First turn the bottom nut to where it stops. Then adjust the first upper nut for the desired amount of play, and fix it in place with the second upper nut (the upper upper one, that is).

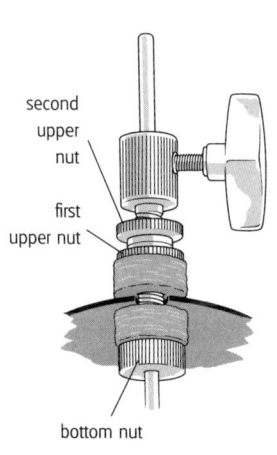

A basic hi-hat clutch.

Stop

A piece of carpet is all you need to keep your bass drum and hi-hat from creeping. Use short-pile carpet. The softer the carpet is, the more it'll muffle your sound. The minimum size is dictated by the surface you need for your throne, your bass drum, your hi-hat and any extra pedals. Left home without a carpet? Use a piece of rope to tie your pedals to your throne. Want to save time setting up?

Use tape (removable) or paint (unremovable) to mark the positions of stands, pedals, and drums on the carpet.

Left or right?
If you happen to be left-handed, you can go for a variety of solutions.
- You can **mirror the entire setup** as shown below. This may be awkward if you share the instrument with others, though, and it makes it harder to sit in: Most sets are configured for right-handed drummers.

... mirror the entire setup...

- As an alternative, **just move the ride cymbal** to the left side of the set. Some right-handed drummers do that too, having trained themselves to keep time with their (initially slower) left hand. Why? Because this way they don't have to cross their arms anymore, as all right-handed drummers have to when keeping time with their right hand on the hi-hat – which is on their left side.
- Teach yourself to play a regular 'right-handed' set, **just as left-handed piano players and sax players** (to name just two examples) play regular 'right-handed' instruments.

MAINTENANCE AND CLEANING
Keeping your drums in good working order is largely a matter of checking the nuts and bolts. When changing heads, check the bolts that keep the lugs in place. Never

over-tighten them, as that'll restrict the vibrations of the shell. Loose-fitting parts may start buzzing and rattling. Are you about to record? Then double-check your entire set for any unwanted sounds – and be prepared to come across sounds that seem to originate from nowhere.

Oil
A few tiny drops of oil once in a while make your pedals move more smoothly. Stiff or jerky tension rods can be cured the same way, unless you're dealing with jagged washers (often overlooked), tension rods, or lug nuts.

More checks
Have a look at the snare strings or straps, and replace them when they show signs of wearing out. The same goes for the sleeves on your cymbal stands. Have a look at your pedals too, and check if everything is as tight or as loose as it's supposed to be. Also check for play in parts that are not supposed to move, and consult your dealer if you find any.

Cleaning
A soft cloth is all you need to keep your instrument shiny, if you use it frequently. Glass cleaners work fine on covered drums. There are special cleaners for drums with lacquered, stained, waxed, or oiled shells; consult your dealer if you're in doubt. Regular furniture cleaners may leave a greasy residue on your shells.

Cymbals
Use chrome polish for chrome-plated parts only, and never on cymbals. If you want to be on the safe side, use genuine cymbal cleaners only, following the instructions on the packaging closely. Some cymbal cleaners are more abrasive than others. A few brands offer special cleaners for B20 or B8 bronze, the latter being less abrasive. Household detergents and water are good for cleaning cymbals, but don't make them shine. Always rinse and dry your cymbals thoroughly when you've finished cleaning.

ON THE ROAD
Here are some important tips for when you take your set on the road.

CHAPTER 10

- Treat your instruments to a set of **gig bags** or **cases**, preferably the ones that have some kind of shock-absorbing lining. Bags, which usually have shoulder straps, are easier to carry than most cases. Gig bags and fiber cases are not always waterproof. Plastic cases are, but they're heavier and often cost more. Hard-shell **flight cases** are very good, very heavy and quite expensive.

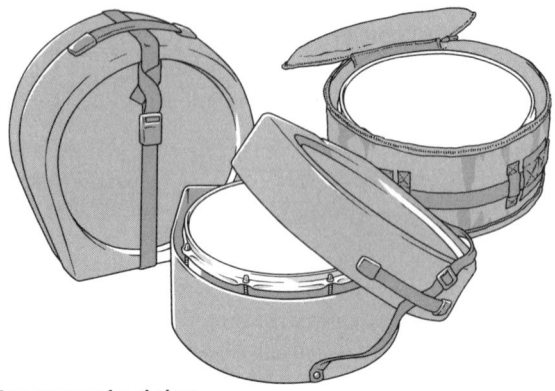

Two cases and a gig bag.

- Your **cymbals need to be packed** too, more than any other part of your set. For one thing, the edges are very vulnerable. Some bags offer extra protection in that area. Cases usually have a center bolt, which keeps the edges from being damaged.
- Cymbal bags usually come with **separators**, which keep your cymbals from scratching each other. A shoulder strap is almost a must.

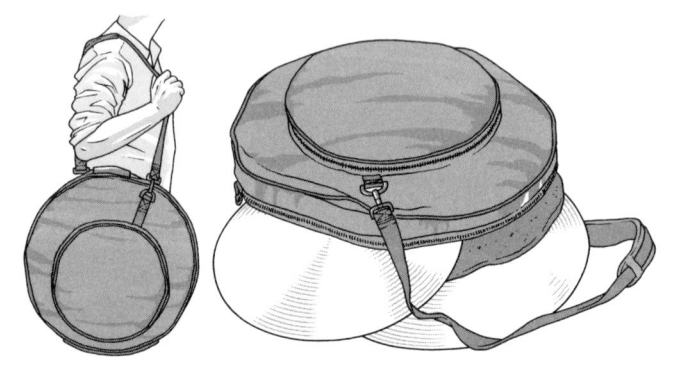

A cymbal bag with separators between the cymbals, handles, and an adjustable shoulder strap.

98

SETTING UP AND MAINTENANCE

- Always have **spare heads** with you, at least for your snare (batter, but snare-side head as well!) and bass drum (batter). Simply keep them in the corresponding cases or bags, or in your car (with your spare tire, for instance).
- Put some **extra sticks and brushes** in you car, just in case you happen to arrive at a gig without your stick bag.
- Brushes don't break, but they can **let go of their wires** all of a sudden – so bring a spare set.
- **Other items to bring**: snare strings or straps, a pair of pliers, a screwdriver, duct tape (for muffling, eliminating rattles and emergency repairs), cymbal sleeves, washers, tension rods, felt washers, and a spare clutch (check to see if it fits your pull rod; they come in different sizes). If possible, also bring a spare bass drum pedal.
- Want to **set up fast**? Use hose clamps on hardware items that don't come with memory locks.
- If you play amplified most of the time, you might consider buying **your own microphones**. There are special drummer's mics that attach to the hoops, and systems to attach mics inside the shells.
- If drums have **serial numbers**, you'll usually find them on the badge. Jot them down (see page 130). Some cymbals have serial numbers, too.
- Consider **insuring your instrument**, especially if you take it on the road. Musical instruments fall under the insurance category of 'valuables'. A regular homeowner insurance policy will not cover all possible damage, whether it occurs at home, on the road, in the studio or onstage.
- **Never** leave your instruments unattended in a car. Ever.

11. BACK IN TIME

The human voice is undoubtedly the oldest instrument around. Drums come second. The drum set, however, is a recent invention. And cymbals? They go back hundreds of years.

It didn't take mankind very long to find out that hitting things sounds good, and hitting hollow things sounds even better. Hollow tree trunks, for instance. Presumably, the drum was born on the day that someone stretched an animal skin over the top of a hollow tree trunk and struck it. Since that day, hundreds of drums and percussion instruments have been invented.

Two drummers
The very first jazz bands had two drummers. One played the snare drum. The second played the bass drum with one hand and the predecessor of the hi-hat with the other: The bottom cymbal, mounted on top of the drum, was played by simply hitting it with the top cymbal.

The pedals
Around 1909, William F. Ludwig came up with the first modern bass drum pedal, which allowed one drummer to play bass and snare drums simultaneously. A second beater rod hit a small cymbal mounted to the side of the pedal. This primitive device eventually made way for the low-hat, a lower version of today's hi-hat. It took another twenty-odd years for someone to lengthen the tube, raising the cymbals to a height where they could be played with sticks as well.

Toms

The early drummers used so-called Chinese toms, which had tacked-on heads. Tunable toms were introduced some time in the mid-1930s, and drum sets haven't changed all that much since then.

Carlton Ridgmount Console from 1935. Note the rack (on wheels!), the cowbells, the temple blocks, and the T-rods on the toms, with tacked on bottom heads. Collection of the Classic Drum Museum, England.

Heads

One of the few major changes in the history of the drum set came in the late 1950s when plastic drum heads slowly started to replace the traditional calf skin heads. Calf skin sounds great, but plastic heads are more consistent and reliable, and plastic is not sensitive to humidity. Calf skin heads, by contrast, need to be retuned practically the moment somebody in a wet coat enters the club you're playing in.

Twenty sizes

The first cymbals were very thick and heavy, and were used in all kinds of rituals and processions, and in military music. The modern cymbal was born in Turkey in 1623, credited to Avedis Zildjian I. Names like ride, crash and splash came much, much later. A 1948 catalog, for instance, simply mentions twenty different sizes (from 7" to 26") in six different weights, from Paper Thin to Heavy.

12. THE PERCUSSION FAMILY

The word percussion comes from the Latin word for hitting. Every instrument that you play by hitting it is part of the percussion family. The number of family members easily runs into thousands. The following chapter mentions some popular examples.

When drummers talk about percussionists, they usually refer to *Latin* percussionists, playing any combination of instruments such as congas, bongos, timbales, cowbells, shakers, rattles, scrapers – and more. The main hand drums are the tall congas and the much shallower, high-pitched bongos. Bongos are always played in pairs. Congueros often use two congas, and sometimes three or more. Most congas and bongos still come with animal skin heads, but plastic heads are gaining acceptance.

Timbales
Timbales are typical Latin-American drums: They resemble snare drums with single plastic heads, which are played with sticks, always in combination with one or more cowbells, and usually a cymbal.

Symphonic and concert drums
In symphony orchestras and concert bands, there's often a separate musician for every percussion instrument. The tympani, for instance, with big, spherical copper shells and single heads that are tuned to specific pitches. Concert bass drums measure up to 40" and more. Cymbals are often played in pairs. If not, they're referred to as *suspended cymbals*.

Marching bands

Marching drummers also play one instrument each. The snare drums are often very deep and tuned extremely high. Single-headed timp-toms, mounted on harnesses, take the place of the drummer's toms. Of course, there's a separate bass drummer too.

timbales with cowbells

congas

Electronic drumming

Electronic drums have more and more to offer each year, in sound, playability, and features. Most electronic drum pads today have tunable heads that feel like 'real' drums. What you play is picked up by built-in triggers that activate digitally recorded sounds (*samples*). The *sound module* allows for many ways of adapting these sounds to your liking (*editing*). Electronic drums are great – though often expensive – for silent practicing, and they're popular in studios as well.

Acoustic, yet digital

Samples can also be activated from your acoustic drum set, either by using triggers on your regular drums, or by using additional pads. Some companies produce special small pads, designed to be added to a drum set.

Drum machines

Most drummers feel that drum machines are operated, rather than played. They can be used to practice with

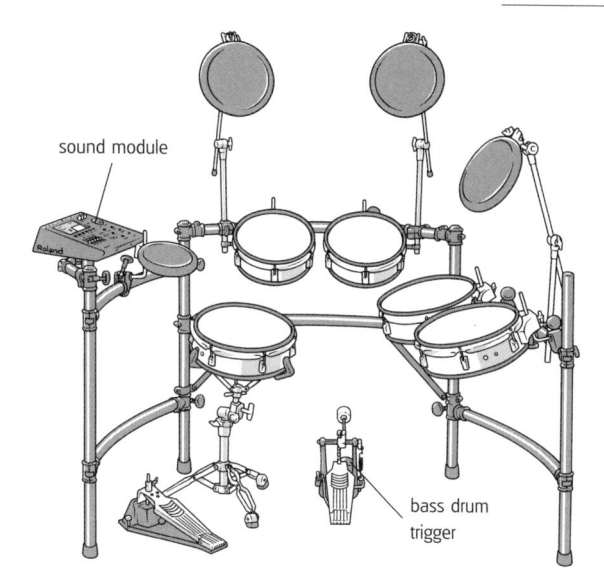

An electronic drum set (Roland).

(they're more fun than a metronome), and in studio situations.

Mallet instruments

Melodic percussion instruments have metal or wooden keys arranged in a way similar to piano keyboards and are played with mallets – hence their other name, mallet instruments. If you play jazz, the family member you're most likely to come across is the vibraphone; its metal keys have resonators with rotating metal discs that generate the vibrating sound. Marimbas and xylophones have wide and narrow wooden keys, respectively. Marching musicians use lyras, with small, bright-sounding metal keys.

Different drums

Hundreds of cultures have their own drums, bells, gongs, and other ethnic percussion instruments. Some of them have been adapted to the demands of Western percussionists. The *djembé*, for instance, is a very popular African, rope-tensioned drum. Western variations have a tuning system that you also find on congas, a similarly built wood or fiberglass shell, and often a plastic head. Another African drum that has been adapted is the talking drum. You hold this drum under your upper arm and by clenching your arm

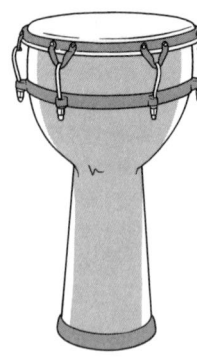

A modern djembé.

you tighten the ropes that connect the two heads. The resulting pitch differences are a language of their own. Some other examples of popular instruments are Brazilian drums ranging from the low *surdo* to the high-pitched *repinique*, the Latin American *cajon* (a wooden case that you both sit and play on), and all kinds of single-headed frame drums, which look like big tambourines without jingles.

Big drums

Traditional Japanese drummers use sticks as thick as your wrist. The biggest Japanese drum, the *odaiko*, is cut out of an enormous tree and weighs close to five hundred pounds. The world's biggest bass drum was much lighter: Built in 1997 by the Dutch company Vancore, this drum featured 165" heads.

TIPBOOK DRUMS

13. HOW THEY'RE MADE

There are many different ways to make drums, cymbals, heads, and sticks: completely by hand, using computer-controlled machines, or anything in between. This chapter gives you a basic idea of the various manufacturing processes.

Tipcode DRUMS-022

One of the main things you need to make a regular plywood drum is a mold – which easily costs as much as a decent car. Most drums are made up of wooden sheets that consist of three plies each, the grains running in alternating directions (*cross laminating*). These sheets are cut to very exact sizes, glued, and then pressed around the inside of the mold. The drying process is usually sped up using heat or microwave technology. When the shells come out, they are cut to length and the bearing edges are cut and sanded.

Pressing the wood around the inside of the mold.

The finish

Lacquered drums wear many coats: stain, color, and one or more clear, protective coats. Shells are sanded or polished after every coat. The cover on covered drums is applied using glue or double-sided adhesive tape. After the shell has been drilled, the drum can be assembled. Not all drum manufacturers produce their own shells, and most do not make their own lugs, hoops, and other metal parts.

CYMBALS
Tipcode DRUMS-023

Cymbals basically start out as flat, round discs. For their B20 cymbals (see page 71), most companies cast their own bronze, producing thick, round castings, one for each cymbal and rolling them down to flat discs in multiple steps. For most other cymbals the flat discs are made elsewhere. UFIP use molds that already have the basic shape of a cymbal.

The shape

Traditionally, cymbals are shaped using hammers. Only few, mostly smaller companies still do this entirely by hand. Most manufacturers use either mechanical hammers (rotating the cymbal under the hammer by hand),

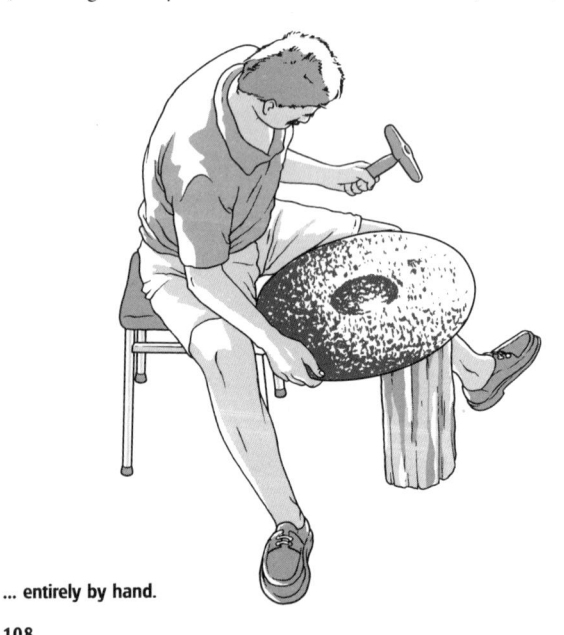

... entirely by hand.

automatic hammers, or computer-controlled hammers. The latter are even used for 'hand-hammered' cymbals in some cases. Sometimes, the cymbals are given an initial shape by pressing them before hammering. The cup is nearly always made by a press.

Spinforming
Many less expensive cymbals are *spinformed*: They are forced in shape against a rotating die. These cymbals are often recognizable by a wide, continuous, even groove on one side. In the late 1990s, some companies started using this technique on B20 cymbals too.

Lathing
The fine grooves that you see on many cymbals are created on a lathe, the worker (or a machine) moving a hardened knife over the surface of the rotating cymbal. This process makes the cymbals shine and opens up the sound. Unlathed cymbals have a 'tighter' sound, generally speaking. A buffing process may be involved as a final step.

Finish
Most cymbals are finished with an ultra-thin coating, making them less susceptible to fingerprints and other stains. The coating is generally said not to influence the sound, and it disappears over the years – or even sooner if you use a cymbal cleaner.

STICKS
Wooden sticks start out as timber that has been cured and cut down to square dowels about one inch across. A grindstone, or a knife with a blade in the shape of a stick, removes exactly the right amount of wood along the length of the rotating dowel. One way of finishing the sticks is to put hundreds of them in a big barrel and throw in some lacquer or wax. Then spin the barrel for a while, and you're done.

HEADS
Basically, there are two ways of making heads. Remo, Evans, and Aquarian use a kind of resin to 'glue' the heads

inside the flesh hoop. Other companies fold the head around a square rod inside the flesh hoop before clamping it down. In all cases, the heads are cut out of large sheets of film, with the collar being formed using heated presses.

14. BRANDS

In this chapter you'll meet some of the main drum and cymbal brands, and a few smaller ones too*. Some of the drum brands sell in all price ranges, others concentrate either on the lower or the higher end of the market. The few large cymbal companies offer a large range of instruments as well. Most smaller ones sell higher-budget cymbals only.

DRUMS

There are eight major brands offering a variety of drum series in pretty much every price range, from low-budget to high-end instruments. Over the years, new brands may be added to this list, while others may have to disappear.

For many years Drum Workshop concentrated on the high-end market with both pedals and drums. With the introduction of the Pacific division in 2000, the products of the company became available in lower price ranges too.

Ludwig goes back more than ninety years. It was this company that introduced the first modern bass drum pedal in 1909. Other legendary designs are the Supra-phonic snare drum and the Speed King bass drum pedal.

---

* *Trademarks and/or user names have been used in this book solely to identify the products or instruments discussed. Such use does not identify endorsement by or affiliation with the trademark owner(s).*

111

CHAPTER 14

MAPEX The Taiwanese Mapex brand came on the scene in the early 1990s and is the latest addition to this group. The company had been making parts and drums for other brands for many years prior to introducing their own drums under the Mapex name.

Pearl One of Pearl's claims to fame is the Pearl Export, the world's best-selling drum set ever. In 1995, the one millionth set was made. Pearl built their first drums in Japan in 1950. Their basic tom holder and bass drum spur designs have been widely copied.

PREMIER Premier has been around since 1922. Numerous classic Premier innovations, from double lugs to convertible boom stands and collapsible lugs, were introduced subsequently as novelties by other companies. Premier makes classic and marching instruments too.

REMO Drummer Remo Belli was one of the pioneers of the plastic drum head in 1957. The Remo company later introduced the wood-resin based Acousticon as the shell material for its own drums. Acousticon is also used for percussion instruments.

SONOR Sonor (Germany, 1875), the oldest company in this list, has long been known for making pretty much every part in-house, and for its continued use of slotted tension rods – which were discontinued on their low-budget, Asian-made sets around 2000.

TAMA The original name of this Japanese brand, Star, is still part of the names of all their series. Tama has always played a major role in hardware developments, such as the boom stand, the multi-clamp, and the 'basket-less' Air Ride snare stand.

YAMAHA Yamaha is one of the largest companies in the music industry, producing a large number of other instruments as well as drums, not to mention motor cycles, hi-fi systems, sailboats, and other products. Few modern sets have been on the market as long as their Recording Custom series, introduced in 1975.

Elsewhere
Most of the companies above also have instruments or parts made in other countries; Taiwan, China, Korea, or Indonesia, for instance – but also in Europe.

US drum companies
Gretsch and **Slingerland** are two of the older US companies. Their first instruments date back to 1883 and 1921, respectively. Both companies offer mainly professional drums. **Rogers**, another brand with a long history, built its last US sets in 1983.

BUDGET PRICE RANGE
Many brands only or mainly offer drum sets in the budget and lower-medium price ranges. Some of these brand names belong to Asian companies, others are owned by American companies that have their instruments made in Asian countries such as Taiwan and Korea. A few better-known examples are **CB Percussion**, **Cannon Percussion**, **Coda**, **Dixon**, **Peace**, **Rockwood**, **Sunlite**, and **Taye**. Some of these companies offer a wider range of instruments and feature more original designs than others.

Your own brand
As with any other type of instrument, more or less anyone can have his own brand of drums made. As long as the order is big enough, you can simply pick a shell design, select the lugs, hoops, holders, and spurs, have a logo and a badge designed, and a new brand is born – often offering good value for money, as little is spent on research and development, or on endorsements.

HIGH-END
If you want the best gear money can buy, you can either look at the high-end series of the brands listed earlier, or at one of the companies that concentrate on high-end

instruments only. What does 'high-end' mean? Well, consider buying a single bass drum for the price of three or four low-budget five-piece drum sets...

Shells and hardware
Hardly any of the high-end companies make their own shells, nor their own hardware. Their main activities are design, research, and development, besides assembling and finishing the drums. More often than not, the shells will be supplied by Keller or Jasper (two US furniture companies, which offer shells in pretty much any configuration).

US
Some of the main high-end US brand names are **GMS**, **Grover**, **Innovation Drum**, **Lang**, **Montineri**, **Noble & Cooley**, **Pork Pie Percussion**, and **Spaun**. A complete listing of US drum brands would include dozens of names.

Other countries
The number of high-end drum companies in other countries is considerably smaller, but they certainly do exist. One of the better known ones is **Ayotte** from Canada, with a special tuning system, hardware made in-house, and its own Wood Hoop drums. England has **Noonan**, Greece has **Gabriel**, and France has **Capelle**. **Brady** and **Sleishman** are made in Australia. In Italy, **Le Soprano** and **Tamburo** produce stave drums.

Specialty drums
Some companies build drums that are different in one way or another. Some examples? In 1997, **Arbiter** (England) introduced its Advanced Tuning System, which uses only one tuning bolt per head. **Peavey**, well-known for its amps and guitars, produces several series of drums with its patented Radial Bridge system. **Fibes** (Plexiglas), **Rocket** (carbon fiber), and **Impact** (fiberglass) are some of the companies that use alternative shell materials.

CYMBAL BRANDS
As basic as a cymbal looks, making one is not at all easy – and that's just one of the reasons why the number of factories producing them is very small.

BRANDS

istanbUL Mehmet — Handmade cymbals from Turkey.
Bosphorus
TURKISH
istanbUL Agop

The Turkish city of Istanbul is where the modern cymbal was born, nearly four centuries ago. The Istanbul company was founded in the early 1980s. Twenty years later, the number of cymbal factories in the city had risen to six: **Anatolian**, **Bosphorus**, **Istanbul Agop**, **Istanbul Mehmet**, and **Turkish Cymbals**. In later years, even more companies introduced handmade Turkish cymbals, including **Agean**, **Amedia**, **Masterwork**, and **TRX**. **Alchemy** cymbals are made by Istanbul Agop.

MEINL The German Meinl brand was founded in 1953. For many years, the company concentrated on the lower end of the market. In the late 1990s, Meinl's professional ranges started growing, and the company largely expanded its range of percussion instruments.

PAiSTe The Swiss cymbal makers at Paiste made their name with the classic 2002 series, which is still around. In the late 1980s they introduced the Paiste Sound Alloy, a new alloy for professional cymbals. Paiste has always been widely represented in all price ranges.

SABIAN Sabian (Canada) made their debut with two series of professional cymbals in 1981, gradually expanding the number of series ever since, in all price-ranges.
Sabian is one of the few factories to make *signature* cymbals, which are developed in co-operation with well-known drummers.

TOSCO Having been an Italian brand from 1974 to 1986, Tosco started a second life in Canada in 1999, with a limited, single series of professional cymbals.

UFiP A merger of a number of small Italian cymbal makers led to the establishment of UFIP in 1931. There's still a lot of handwork involved in their professional series, which were thoroughly revised in the 1990s.

The Zildjian company dates back to 1623, when the Armenian Avedis Zildjian discovered how to treat bronze in such a way that you could make great cymbals out of it. Even after more than 375 years, the current president is still a direct descendant of Avedis Zildjian.

MORE CYMBALS

As with drums and other instruments, there are more cymbal brands than there are manufacturers. **Camber** and **Headliner**, made by manufacturers mentioned above, are just two of the better-known examples. Low-budget Asian drum sets often come with Asian cymbals that either carry no name, or the brand name of the drums. Small professional cymbal shops are very rare. One of them is **Spizz** (Italy), under whose name a series of low-budget cymbals is also produced.

China

Most Chinese cymbals come from the province of **Wuhan**, where cymbals are still made the way they were decades ago.

15. SETUPS

A drum set can be as big or as small as you like – from just a bass drum, a snare drum, a hi-hat, and a single cymbal to setups with three or more bass drums, and anything in between. The four examples in this chapter are just that: examples. After all, the definitive rock drum set is just as imaginary as the definitive rock drummer.

BASIC, STANDARD FIVE-PIECE SETUP

Most drummers start on this basic, five-piece set – and many stick to it. Combined with a similarly basic cymbal setup, this is an instrument that will do in a wide variety of styles. A second crash cymbal, to the left of the ride, is often one of the first additions.

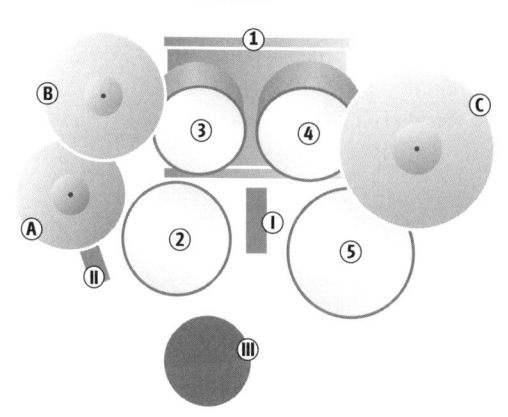

1. 16x22 bass drum
2. 6.5x14 snare drum
3. 10x12 power tom
4. 11x13 power tom
5. 16x16 floor tom

A. 14" hi-hats
B. 16" or 18" crash cymbal
C. 20" ride cymbal

I. bass drum pedal
II. hi-hat stand
III. drum throne

NINE-PIECE ROCK SETUP

The louder the music, the bigger the drums, and the bigger and heavier the cymbals. Cymbals for hard-hitting drummers usually come with names like rock crashes, power rides, and heavy hi-hats. Two-ply heads, which dent less easily, are the most popular choice. The tuning is generally on the low side.

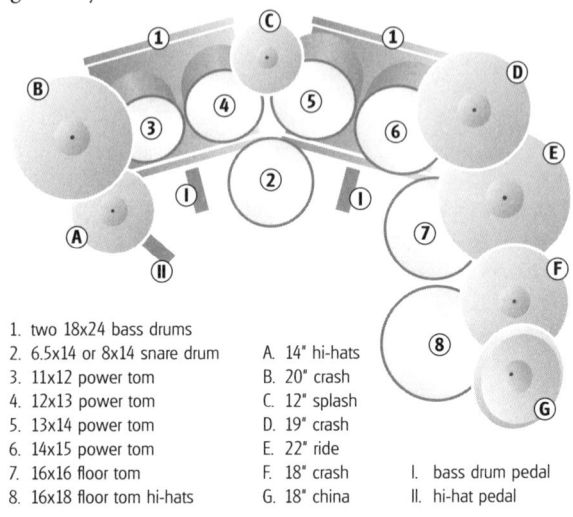

1. two 18x24 bass drums
2. 6.5x14 or 8x14 snare drum
3. 11x12 power tom
4. 12x13 power tom
5. 13x14 power tom
6. 14x15 power tom
7. 16x16 floor tom
8. 16x18 floor tom hi-hats

A. 14" hi-hats
B. 20" crash
C. 12" splash
D. 19" crash
E. 22" ride
F. 18" crash
G. 18" china

I. bass drum pedal
II. hi-hat pedal

FOUR-PIECE JAZZ SETUP

Many jazz drummers use four-piece sets in small sizes, often combined with two or three fairly thin, big, dark-sounding cymbals that are used both for crashing and timekeeping. One of these cymbals often has three or more rivets. The drums generally have coated, one-ply heads, often tuned to a high pitch.

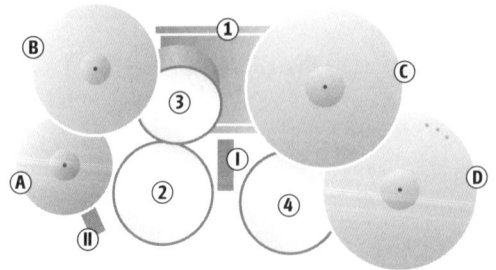

1. 14x18 bass drum
2. 5x14 snare drum
3. 8x12 tom
4. 14x14 floor tom

A. 14" hi-hats
B. 18" or 20" cymbal
C. 22" cymbal
D. 22" sizzle cymbal (three rivets)

I. bass drum pedal
II. hi-hat stand

EIGHT-PIECE FUSION SETUP

Fusion is a kind of cross between rock and jazz, and that shows in the typical fusion setup. The drums are smaller than those of the average rock set, but there are more drums than a jazz drummer might use. Similar things can be said about the cymbals and the tuning, both of which are designed to supply a bit more power and definition than jazz drummers normally choose. Heads can be either one- or two-ply. Note the second snare, the mounted 'floor' toms, cowbell, double bass drum pedal, and remote hi-hat pedal III, which is used to operate the hi-hat cymbals on the right (G).

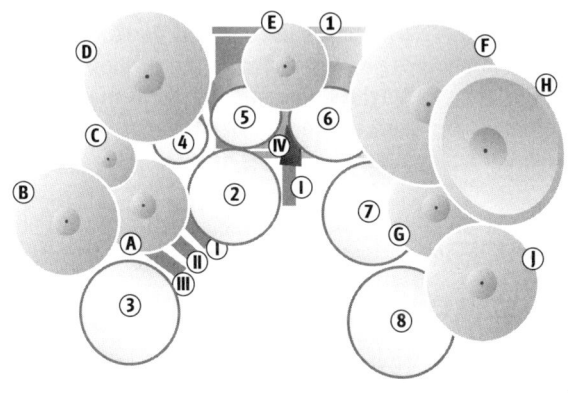

1. 16x20 bass drum
2. 3.5x13 piccolo
3. 6.5x14 snare drum
4. 7x8 tom
5. 8x10 tom
6. 9x12 tom
7. 11x14 suspended tom
8. 12x15 suspended tom

A. 13" hi-hats
B. 15" crash
C. 8" splash
D. 18" crash
E. 12" splash
F. 22" ride
G. 14" remote hi-hats
H. 22" china
I. 16" crash

I. double pedal
II. hi-hat pedal
III. remote hi-hat pedal
IV. cowbell

GLOSSARY AND INDEX

This glossary contains short definitions of all the drum- and cymbal-related terms used in this book. There are also some words you won't find in the previous pages, but which you might well come across in magazines, catalogs, and books. The numbers refer to the pages where the terms are used in this book.

Acousticon *(27)* A wood-resin based shell material.

Action See: *Snare strainer.*

Base plate *(50)* Stabilizing plate for bass drum and hi-hat pedals.

Bass drum *(5–7, 36–39)* Your largest drum, played with a bass drum pedal.

Bass drum pedal *(3, 4, 6, 47–52)* The pedal you play the bass drum with. *Double pedals* allow you to use two feet to play one drum, removing the need for a second bass drum.

Batter head See: *Heads.*

Bead See: *Tip.*

Bearing edge *(28–29)* The edge of a shell, which 'bears' the head.

Beater *(51)* Beats the bass.

Bell See: *Cup.*

Boom stand *(9, 57)* Cymbal stand with an extra arm.

Bracket *(5)* The arms of a tom holder and the legs of a floor tom are held in place with brackets.

Brushes *(68–69)* Brushing drums with steel or nylon strands produces a *shhhhh* sound. Also known as *wire brushes.*

Chinese cymbal *(75, 76)* Cymbal with a turned-up

120

edge. Also available in a lot of Western variations.

Clutch *(53–54, 95)* Secures your top hi-hat cymbal to the pull rod.

Concert toms *(46)* Single-headed toms; also known as *melodic toms*.

Counter hoop See: *Hoop*.

Crash, crash cymbal *(8, 74–75)* Fast-speaking cymbals, mainly used for accenting and adding color to the music.

Cup *(8–9, 71, 73, 76)* The little 'bulge' in the middle of a cymbal, also known as the *bell*, often used for penetrating ride patterns in Latin rhythms.

Cymbals *(8–9, 21–22, 70–77)* Deceptively simple-looking discs, usually made of bronze, available in hundreds of sizes, shapes, types, and thicknesses.

Dampening See: *Muffling*.

Dot *(61–62)* A thin, circular piece of drum head material on a drum head. Dries out the sound and helps resist denting.

Double-braced *(9, 55, 56)* Double-braced stands have legs that are made up of two metal strips, instead of one.

Double pedal See: *Bass drum pedal*.

Drop-lock clutch *(54)* Type of clutch that allows you to 'drop' the top cymbal onto the bottom cymbal.

Drum key *(79)* T-shaped tool for tuning drums; also available in speed versions and ratchet versions.

Drum machine *(18–19, 104–105)* Programmable electronic 'drum set' or *drum computer*.

Drum rack *(57–58)* Replaces the bottom sections of cymbal stands, microphone stands, and so on. Especially useful for larger setups.

Electronic drums *(16, 104, 105)* A series of pads with built-in electronic components that pick up your playing, triggering sounds that are stored in a sound module. These sounds are mostly digitally recorded (samples).

Flesh hoop *(29, 30, 110)* The hoop of a drum head (usually made of aluminum).

Floating heads *(30)* Drums with slightly undersized shells have floating heads.

Floor tom *(4, 7, 41)* Three-legged drum, most popular in 16x16.

Flush bracing See: *Lugs*.

Fusion set *(7, 119)* Fusion is a musical mixture of rock and jazz elements, which led to the creation of the fusion drum set, usually featuring 10" and 12" rack toms and suspended floor toms.

Hardware *(9–10, 20–21, 47–59)* Stands, pedals, holders, and racks, plus the lugs, tension rods, washers, bolts and all other metal items – except for the cymbals.

Heads *(4–5, 22–23, 43–44, 46, 60–64, 80, 84, 109–110)* Drum heads are made of one or two thin plies of polyester film, the sound being determined by their thickness and by additional coatings, dots, fillings, holes and/or built-in muffling rings, to name just a few. Most drums have two heads: a *top* or *batter* head and a *bottom* or *resonant* head (called *snare-side head* on snare drums, *front head* on bass drums).

Hickory *(66)* Most popular type of wood for sticks. And hammer handles. And hockey sticks. And more.

High-tension lugs See: *Lugs*.

Hi-hat *(3, 10)* Two cymbals of equal size (hi-hat cymbals; *73–74, 95*) and a stand with a pedal (hi-hat pedal; *10*) that operates them. Almost always found by a drummer's left foot.

Hoop Drums are tuned by using the hoops to tighten the head over the shell. Also known as counter hoops. See also: *Flesh hoop, Triple-flanged hoops*.

Isolated mounting system *(43, 83)* Isolates drums (rack toms, especially) from their mounting hardware, enhancing their sound and resonance. Introduced by Gary Gauger. His RIMS are regarded as one of the few major innovations in drums in recent decades.

Key bolts, key rods See: *Tension rods*.

Lathed cymbals *(71, 109)* Most cymbals are lathed. The lathing knife creates the circular pattern of grooves on the cymbal's surface, opening up its sound.

GLOSSARY AND INDEX

Unlathed cymbals have a tighter sound.

Left-handed drummers *(10, 96)* Left-handed drummers have quite a number of alternative options.

Lug bolts See: *Tension rods.*

Lugs, lug casings *(5, 33, 46)* Metal casings which house the lug nuts into which the tension rods are screwed. Also known as *tension mounts*. If a drum is said to have *flush bracing*, *long lugs*, *double lugs*, or *high-tension lugs*, this means that each lug receives a tension rod from both the batter and the resonant head. See also: *Nodal points.*

Mallets *(69, 105)* Sticks with large heads, usually covered with felt (tympani mallets) or wound with yarn (xylophone mallets, for instance). If someone plays *mallets*, they play mallet instruments such as the vibraphone and the marimba *(105)*.

Melodic toms See: *Concert toms.*

Memory locks *(42, 54, 99)* Metal clamps that help you set up fast. Originally a trade name – other names include *key locks* and *stop locks.*

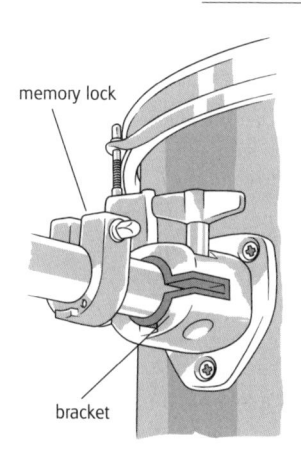

Memory lock on a tom holder.

Metronome *(18)* Helps you to keep steady time.

Muffling *(87–92)* There are many different ways of muffling or dampening your drums, which controls the tone to some extent.

Multi-clamp *(58)* Used to clamp holders to stands or racks.

Mylar *(62)* Widely-used (Dupont) trade name for the polyester film that drum heads are made of.

Nodal points Drum shells are said to have nodal points, indicating positions at which there is no vibration. It is claimed that mounting lugs and brackets on those spots enhances the drum's resonance. Not all experts agree on this issue – but what else is new...

Oil *(63)* Two-ply heads often look as though they have oil between the plies, though they don't in most cases.

O-ring *(63, 90–92)* Ring cut out of the film that heads are made of. Popular for muffling snare drums.

Pad *(15–16)* The most basic pad is a wooden plank with a slice of rubber on top, enabling silent practice. See also: *Electronic drums*.

Ported bass drum head *(89)* Bass drum front head with a hole.

Power toms *(40)* Toms with extra deep shells; like power cymbals they're primarily designed for heavy players.

Practice pad See: *Pad*.

Pull rod *(53)* The rod to which you attach the top cymbal of your hi-hat. It 'pulls' the top down towards the bottom cymbal.

Rack *(57–58)* Drum rack; hardware system that replaces the bottom sections of cymbal stands and other stands.

Rack toms *(7, 39–41)* Common name for the smaller toms, which are mounted on the bass drum or on a drum rack.

Reinforcement hoops *(29–30)* Wooden rings around the edges of a drum. They reinforce the shell and also influence the sound.

Remote hi-hat *(55)* Hi-hat pedal with a long cable connecting the pedal to the top section. Often used for a second pair of hi-hat cymbals on the right side of the set. See also: *X-hat*.

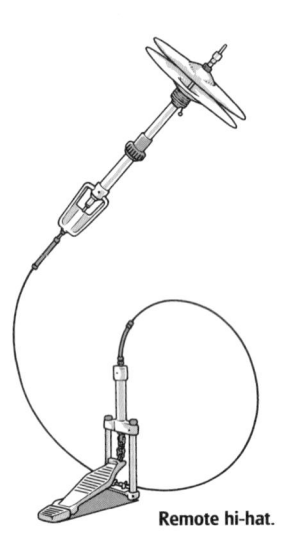

Remote hi-hat.

Resonant head See: *Heads*.

Ride cymbal *(3, 4, 8, 72–73)* Usually the heaviest and largest cymbal of the set, primarily used for time-keeping – you play time (the *ride*) on it.

RIMS See: *Isolated mounting system.*

Rivets *(75)* Inserting one or more rivets into a cymbal will turn it into a sizzle cymbal.

Seamless shells Some snare drums and hoops are seamless, meaning their shape is forced out of a flat metal disc, thus eliminating the need for a welded seam.

Shell *(4, 5, 26–31)* The sound chamber of a drum. If you take every single component (heads, lugs, etc.) off your drum, all you'll be left with is the shell.

Shell set, shell kit *(20)* A set sold without any stands or pedals.

Single lugs See: *Lugs.*

Sizzle cymbal *(75)* Cymbal with rivets, producing a 'sizzling' sound.

Snare, snare drum *(3, 6, 7, 34–36)* One of the two main drums of the drum set. Both the drum's name and its sound come from the set of snares against the bottom head.

Snare bed *(36)* Snare drums are a bit shallower where the snare strings or straps run over the edge. This recess, referred to as the snare bed, helps the snares to lie flat against the snare-head over their entire length.

Snare-side head *(36, 62, 85–86)* Bottom head of a snare drum. Very, very thin.

Snare strainer *(6, 7, 35)* Allows you to adjust the tension of the snares, and to disengage them (throw them off) if you wish. Other names include *snare mechanism*, *throw-off*, and *action*.

Snares *(6, 7, 35–36, 85–87)* The spiraled wires (about twenty of them) against the bottom head.

Spring tension *(10, 48, 49–50, 51, 53)* Determines how heavy or light a pedal feels. Adjustable on all bass drum pedals and most hi-hat pedals.

Square drum sizes *(41)* Drums whose depth equals their diameter (*e.g.*, 12x12).

Stands *(9, 55–57)* You use a variety of stands for toms, cymbals, and snare drums, with single- or double-braced legs.

Suspended cymbals *(103)* Symphonic cymbals.

Symmetrical drum sizes See: *Square drum sizes*.

Tension mounts See: *Lugs*.

Tension rods, tension screws, tension bolts *(5, 33, 37–38)* Variety of names for the 'tuning keys' of a drum. Also known as *key rods*, *lug bolts*, or *key bolts*.

Throne *(59)* Drum throne, drum stool.

Throw-off See: *Snare strainer*.

Tilter *(9, 42, 53, 55, 95)* Enables a part of a stand to tilt. You'll find a tilter on all cymbal stands, snare drum stands, tom, and hi-hat pedals. *Ratchet tilters* or *gear tilters* use two sets of interlocking teeth; toothless tilters allow for finer adjustment.

Tips *(66, 67)* Most drumsticks have wooden tips or *beads*, in a wide variety of shapes and sizes. Nylon tips sound brighter, especially on cymbals.

Tom holder *(3, 41–43)* Mount for rack toms.

Tom, tom toms *(7, 39–41)* The 'other' drums, besides your snare drum and bass drum. May either be mounted (rack toms) or on legs (floor toms).

Trigger pad Drum pad with built-in electronics that pick up your beats and send them to the sound module where they trigger sounds. See also: *Electronic drums* and *Pad*.

Triple-flanged hoops Pressed hoops *(31)* usually have three flanges. The upper one, which protects your sticks from the biting effect of rimshots, was added last. So, historically-speaking, it's the third flange.

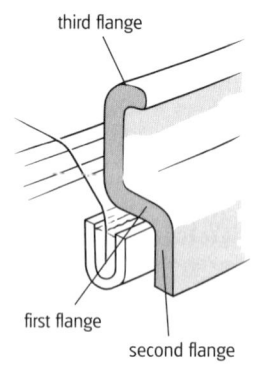

Tuning *(78–88)* Some say you can't tune a drum; all you can do is tighten the heads – but most drummers do use the word tuning.

Wire brushes See: *Brushes*.

X-hat *(55)* Holder for an extra pair of hi-hat cymbals, originally a trade name. See also: *Remote hi-hat*.

TIPCODE LIST

The Tipcodes in this book offer easy access to short movies, photo series, soundtracks, and other additional information at www.tipbook.com. For your convenience, the Tipcodes in this Tipbook have been listed below.

Tipcode	Topic	Chapter	Page
DRUM-001	A five-piece drum set, step by step	2	3
DRUM-002	Basic rock rhythm (audio)	3	13
DRUM-003	Checking the bearing edge	5	30
DRUM-004	Checking the diameter	5	31
DRUM-005	Tom holder w. ball-and-socket joint	5	42
DRUM-006	Setting a memory lock	5	42
DRUM-007	Spring adjustment bass drum pedal	6	48
DRUM-008	Spring adjustment hi-hat pedal	6	53
DRUM-009	Boom stand	6	57
DRUM-010	Adjusting a snare drum stand	6	57
DRUM-011	Removing a muffling ring	7	63
DRUM-012	Lathed/unlathed cymbals	8	71
DRUM-013	Ratchet key	9	79
DRUM-014	Removing drum head (two keys)	9	79
DRUM-015	Basic drum head tension	9	80
DRUM-016	Tuning order	9	80
DRUM-017	Fine tuning	9	81
DRUM-018	Making a bridge for the snares	9	85
DRUM-019	Adjusting an internal muffler	9	92
DRUM-020	Top cymbal and clutch	10	94
DRUM-021	Adjusting the clutch	10	94
DRUM-022	Making of a drum	13	107
DRUM-023	Making of a cymbal	13	108

WANT TO KNOW MORE?

This book gives you all the basics you need for buying, maintaining, tuning, and using drums, cymbals, sticks and drum heads. If you want to know more, try the magazines, books and websites listed below.

MAGAZINES

There are a number of specialized drummers' magazines and e-zines, featuring interviews, product reviews and other articles. You may also find relevant articles in general music magazines.

- *Classic Drummer*, www.classicdrummer.com
- *Drum!*, www.drummagazine.com
- *Drummer Magazine* (UK), www.drummer-mag.com
- *DrumPRO Magazine*, drumpro.com (e-zine)
- *Modern Drummer*, www.moderndrummer.com.
- *Muzik Etc./Drums Etc.* (Canada), www.muziketc.ca
- *Not So Modern Drummer*, www.notsomoderndrummer.com
- *Percussive Notes*, www.pas.org/publications/notes.cfm
- *Rhythm* (UK), www.futurenet.com
- *Tom Girl Magazine*, www.tomgirlmagazine.com (e-zine)
- *Traps, The Art Of Drumming*, www.trapsmagazine.com

BOOKS

Most books on drums deal largely with the history of the instrument, but some titles cover today's instruments as well. The following list contains examples of both.

- *Guide to Vintage Drums*, by John Aldridge (Centerstream, USA, 1996; 174 pages; ISBN 09 3175 979 X).

- *Gretsch Drums – The Legacy of That Great Gretsch Sound*, by Chet Falzerano (Centerstream, USA, 1996; 144 pages; ISBN 09 3175 998 6).
- *History of Leedy Drum Co.: The World's Largest Drum Co.*, by Rob Cook (Centerstream, USA, 1996; 178 pages; ISBN 09 3175 974 9).
- *Star Sets: Drum Kits of the Great Drummers*, by Jon Cohan (Hal Leonard, USA, 1995; 160 pages; ISBN 07 9353 489 5).
- *The Cymbal Book*, by Hugo Pinksterboer (Hal Leonard, USA, 1993; 212 pages; ISBN 07 935 1920 9).
- *The Drum Book, A History of the Rock Drum Kit,* by Geoff Nichols (Balafon, England, 1997; 112 pages; ISBN 1 871 547 25 3).
- *The Drummer's Almanac*, by Jon Cohan (Hal Leonard, USA, 1998; 80 pages; ISBN 07 9356 696 7).
- *The Drummer's Studio Survival Guide*, by Mark Huntley Parsons (Modern Drummer Publications, USA, 1996; 94 pages; ISBN 7935 7222 3).
- *The Great American Drums and the Companies that Made Them*, 1920–1969, by Harry Cangany (Hal Leonard, USA, 1996; 72 pages; ISBN 07 9356 356 9).
- *The Drumset Owner's Manual – A Heavily Illustrated Guide to Selecting, Setting Up and Maintaining All Components of the Acoustic Drumset*, by Ronald Vaughan (McFarland & Company, USA/UK, 1993; 164 pages; ISBN 08 9950 755 7).
- *The Drum Handbook – Buying, Maintaining, and Getting the Best From Your Drum Kit*, Geoff Nichols (Backbeat Books, 2003; 192 pages; ISBN 0-87930-750-1).

INTERNET

The Internet is an excellent source of information on instruments and drummers. Here are some websites to start with:
- www.drummergirl.com
- www.drummerszone.com
- www.drummerworld.com
- www.drums.com
- www.drumset.com
- www.drum-talk.com
- www.drumtips.com
- Percussion Information: www.xs4all.nl/~marcz

ESSENTIAL DATA

In the event of your equipment being stolen or lost, or if you decide to sell it, it's useful to have all the relevant data at hand. Here are two pages to make those notes. For the insurance, for the police, or just for yourself.

INSURANCE

Insurance company:

Phone: Fax:

Broker:

Phone: Fax:

Policy no.:

Premium:

DRUM SET

Make and series:

Color:

Price:

Date of purchase:

Place of purchase:

Phone: Fax:

DRUMS

Sizes, serial numbers, and other relevant data per drum.

1

2

3

4

5

6

7

8

9

10

11

ESSENTIAL DATA

CYMBALS

Brand name, series, size, date of purchase, price, serial number, and/or other data per cymbal. Most cymbals come without a serial number. If it's there, you'll find it on the inside of the cup.

1
2
3
4
5
6
7
8
9
10

ACCESSORIES AND OTHER INSTRUMENTS

1
2
3
4
5
6
7
8

ADDITIONAL NOTES

ADDITIONAL NOTES